Kathy
Crampton

FASHION DOLLS

FASHION DOLLS

Maree Tarnowska

Foreword by Dorothy Coleman
Fashion Notes by Madeleine Ginsburg

HOBBY HOUSE PRESS, INC.
Cumberland, Maryland 21502

First published in the United States and North America in 1986
by Hobby House Press Inc, 900 Frederick Street, Cumberland, Maryland 21502.
(301) 759-3770.

ISBN: 0 87588 286 2

Created, designed and produced by
Black Pig Editions Ltd
(Justin Knowles Publishing Group)
9 Colleton Crescent, Exeter, Devon EX2 4BY

Consultant: Charles Farrow
Design: Roger Huggett
Production: Nick Facer

Publisher's note:
the English spelling of "mannikin" has been used throughout the text instead of "mannequin," which is more usual in the United States.

Typeset by Keyspools Limited
Warrington
Printed and bound in Hong Kong by
Mandarin Offset Ltd

First American Edition

FRONTISPIECE
All we can see clearly of this outfit of c.1885 are the hat and parasol. The complete outfit consists of a hip-length satin bodice with pleated tails, worn over a pleated skirt with an apron drape, made from a beige, figured silk mixture. The 1880s-style hat, of satin trimmed with leather flowers, is labelled

Author's Acknowledgements

I would like to give my sincere thanks to the following for the great assistance I received from them during the time the book was in preparation.

In the United Kingdom Madeleine Ginsburg, who provided the detailed fashion notes that are included in the captions to the colour plates; Jackie Jacobs, who did the unthinkable and allowed me to strip and re-dress those dolls that she loaned to me; and Elsie Potter, for no less reason than Jackie, and who supplied me with a Rochard patent doll.

In the United States Dorothy and Jane Coleman, who were both critical and supportive in equal proportion and who provided invaluable suggestions to help me on my way; Stephanie Farago, who made a number of journeys on my behalf in search of suitable material; Gladys Hillsdorf, who allowed me a completely free run of her magnificent collection; Marshall Martin for information supplied on fashion dolls in his collection; John Noble, the curator of the Museum of the City of New York, and his charming assistant, Jane, who could not have been more helpful; Margaret Whitton, curator of the Margaret Woodbury Strong Museum, who allowed me to examine many exhibits at my leisure; and Richard Wright and Ricky Saxman, who entrusted a single doll to a trans-Atlantic flight in the interests of further research.

In France the curator of the Musée National de Monaco, where I was able to see many fine examples of French fashion dolls.

I would also like to thank the Justin Knowles Publishing Group for its help in producing this book. We had numerous battles, and the only one I regret losing was over the size of the photographs that show undressed dolls.

Above all, however, I should like to thank Charles Farrow, without whose unstinting and continual help and encouragement this book would not have been possible.

"Verey's, Ltd., Manchester" and was probably made in the 1920s. The parasol, which, like the outfit, dates from c.1885, has a faceted glass knob.

MARKS Unmarked. SIZE 23in (58cm). HEAD Swivel neck; grey-blue glass eyes; pierced ears. BODY All leather; no gussets. BODY STYLE N2 (page 130).

CONTENTS

FOREWORD

The term "fashion doll" is used by many doll collectors to designate a particular type of doll – that which originally enjoyed its greatest popularity in the years between 1860 and about 1890. These dolls usually had bisque heads, wigs, and leather- or cloth-covered bodies, shaped to suggest the figure of an adult woman or older girl. When new, these dolls sometimes came fully dressed, occasionally with a trunk full of clothes and accessories, but it was possible also to buy unclothed dolls that did, however, have dressed hair and jewellery, including ear-rings in their pierced ears. If the doll had a swivel neck, it would also wear a bead choker to hide the neck joint.

Bru's 1872 catalogue shows fashion dolls that are naked apart from jewellery, dolls that are wearing chemises and dolls that are completely dressed. Some of the fashion dolls that had been purchased naked were dressed in clothes made at home from published patterns. Many of the magazines published at this time were solely or partly devoted to conveying information about, and illustrations of, the dolls, their dresses and their accessories. In the early 1860s *Dolly's Dressmaker* was published in Berlin, London and the United States. At the same time, the *Journal des Demoiselles* in Paris published patterns for the clothes of a lady named "Miss Lilly," a name later used by the children's magazine, *La Poupée Modèle*, which was published by the same firm and which provided patterns for dolls' clothing and accessories. The name *La Poupée Modèle* may be translated as "The Fashion Doll." *La Poupée Modèle* was produced monthly, beginning in 1863, by Mlle. Peronne, whose shop in the rue de Choiseul, Paris, may have been the one described in the report of the 1867 Paris International Exhibition:

Soon after the Crimean War [there] started a doll's wardrobe shop in the rue de Choiseul.... This shop ... was the parent of at least two hundred establishments of a similar nature which are now [1867] scattered all over Paris.

... dolly required a parasol, a pocket-handkerchief, a reticule, a scent bottle, ... a trunk with a movable tray for her fine linen, ... brushes with ivory backs, ... and a fan when she was warm....

... see what Rémond and Huret ... what Simonne ... all of Paris have to show in the way of dolls and dolls' toilets [*sic*], gutta-percha dolls, wax dolls, articulated wooden dolls, porcelain dolls....

From at least 1862, William Henry Cremer Jr., who was often referred to as Merlin, had a famous toy shop in London. In December 1865 *The English Woman's Domestic Magazine*, a magazine that featured French high fashion, published an article on the dolls and their accessories in the Cremer Toy Store. The following excerpts provide a vivid contemporary picture of early fashion dolls.

... we were freely admitted into all the marvels and mysteries of our little lady's toilet [*sic*].

Here were jewel-boxes, full of brooches and buckles, and ear-rings and bandeaux, and bracelets and chains, and necklaces, and watches, gold and silver, and diamonds and pearls, rubies, emeralds ... and all the rest that are known to the lapidary. ... stays and crinolines (for her dollyship must be in the fashion)....

Merlin kindly showed us the trousseaux of many miniature ladies, all containing everything that a lady can require and many of them everything a lady might desire.

Although the article goes on to say "As to dolly herself, her face and head and neck are made of wax so are her limbs, her body is made of kid," a bisque-head fashion doll has been found with one of Cremer's paper labels on its kid body.

Cremer himself wrote, in 1873, about a doll and its trousseaux costing $400:

> She had several dresses besides, but the most worthy of notice were a dinner dress and a ball dress; . . . The whole of her under-linen was of the finest batiste. . . . She belonged to the class . . . which . . . for more than a hundred years past has shown empresses, queens and ladies of fashion at the courts of Europe how to dress. . . .

With such delights as were to be found in Cremer's shop, it is hardly surprising that he was called "Merlin" – the sorcerer in the Arthurian legend.

The December 1865 issue of *The English Woman's Domestic Magazine* also contained a picture of a dressed "DOLL A LA WATTEAU from an original figure. Expressly designed by JULES DAVID and dressed by CREMER JUNIOR." Jules David, a famous painter and fashion illustrator for *Le Moniteur de la Mode*, a magazine appearing during the latter part of the 19th century, showed dressed dolls in some of his fashion paintings.

Not all fashion dolls originally wore high fashion clothes. Some of the dolls were dressed in garments representing the costumes of various provinces, as well as the city of Paris. None of the dolls illustrated in this book is wearing regional dress, however; most of the dolls shown on the following pages are dressed as ladies, although some wear the garments of older girls, both types of dress being usual for this type of doll. Occasionally these dolls may even be found in their original attire representing males, for only its clothes determined whether the doll represented a grown woman, an older girl or a man: the same type of body was used, regardless of the sex and age indicated by the doll's clothes.

Despite the apparent similarity of fashion dolls, there is a tremendous diversity in detail from doll to doll. Their bisque heads differ in appearance, partly because of the differences in the shape of the features and partly because of variations in the painting – seldom do two heads look exactly alike. Bru, for example, is known to have used at least two different moulds for his fashion dolls, and even dolls from the same mould can differ in appearance because of the changes that take place in the bisque at the greenware stage or during firing. The variation in the shape and structure of the bodies, too, is tremendous, as is excellently demonstrated by the many illustrations of undressed dolls included in this book.

Some of the earlier fashion dolls had glazed china heads, but, around 1860, when bisque-head dolls began to be produced, fashion dolls were among the first type of dolls to have bisque heads. Collectors who, in the 1920s to 1940s, had concentrated on dolls with glazed china heads, turned in the 1950s to collecting bisque-head dolls, and their first choice was the bisque-head fashion doll. In the last quarter of the 19th century, *bébés* or dolls representing children began to supersede fashion dolls, and, similarly, collectors' interest in antique child dolls by the 1970s had tended to supersede their interest in fashion dolls. Now, however, in the late 1980s, there is a growing interest in dolls' clothes, especially in the clothes and accessories of fashion dolls, and modern collectors are finding it hard to resist the magic of these dolls. The elaborately dressed dolls, with their marvellous accessories, seem to belong to a fanciful and intriguing wonder world.

As research continues into the history of fashion dolls and we learn more about their beautiful clothes and accessories, more and more people are beginning to appreciate these lovely treasures from the past. This book, with its outstanding illustrations, cannot fail to intrigue all those with an interest in both dolls and fashion.

Dorothy S. Coleman

INTRODUCTION

Antique dolls are a fascinating subject, and few types of doll have so caught the imagination of collectors everywhere as the bisque-head dolls manufactured in France and Germany between 1860 and 1890. Novice collectors are initially enchanted by the simple beauty of these dolls and the clothes they wear, but, as they delve more deeply into the subject, they soon discover that the range and diversity of type, style, material and manufacture open up a whole new world of interest.

The attraction of *all* antiques has undoubtedly increased in recent years. This is partly because there has been a massive resurgence of interest in items that reflect the standards and values of past generations, and partly perhaps because of a feeling of disillusionment with the prosaic and utilitarian products of our own generation. There are also those, of course, whose chief motivation has been the never-ending search for a "good investment" and nowhere is this better illustrated than in the steep rise in prices paid in the world of fine art.

The price of most antique dolls, including fashion dolls, has also risen steeply, but, fortunately, investment mania has not been the primary reason. To a greater degree it has been the increasing number of collectors chasing a stable number of dolls that has resulted in a fairly consistent upward spiral in these prices. If we discard the desire to invest as the main motive behind such increases we must also accept that it can only be the intrinsic beauty and attraction of antique dolls worldwide that is responsible for their increase in value.

Collectors of fashion dolls may be found in all parts of the world, especially America, Europe and Japan, but there are also enthusiasts in such diverse places as the outback of Australia and the veldt of South Africa. Every state of the union in America has its doll clubs, and most of these are linked to a central body – the United Federation of Doll Clubs. There are fewer clubs in Europe, but the very large number of collectors is reflected in the fact that doll sales, in the form of "doll fairs," are held in many major cities on various occasions throughout the year.

There is a wealth of information about fashion dolls in many places – publications old and new, museums, records of manufacture, archives in patent offices and the knowledge of veteran collectors worldwide – but to add to the excitement of collecting, none of this information is so exact or precise as to be beyond the challenge of later discoveries, which are continually being made. There is still, for example, much disagreement regarding both the historical origins of fashion dolls and their role as children's playthings. Did they fill the needs of a child at play and educate the emerging woman? Did they merely reflect the changing style in fashion of generations?

It would be a very unwise "expert" who claimed to have a complete knowledge of the whole subject. This book is not intended to be the definitive word on the fashion doll; rather it is an attempt to communicate something of the fascination of these dolls; the enchanting combination of the attractive plaything of a child and the exotic gowns displayed by 19th-century women. They are fantasies in miniature and arresting visions – as is beautifully shown by the dolls illustrated in this book. It is hoped that it will meet with the approval of established collectors, and, just as importantly, will enable novices more fully to understand and appreciate these most dignified of dolls.

THE HISTORY OF THE FASHION DOLL

Dolls have existed since earliest times. Man has, it seems, always made images in his own likeness, whether for religious, symbolic, votive or talismanic reasons. There were dolls in ancient Egypt and ancient Greece; dolls at the courts of the wealthy and titled in the Middle Ages; and, as the 18th and 19th centuries saw more relaxed attitudes toward children, dolls as playthings for boys and girls alike.

Fashion dolls, in the sense of dolls produced specifically to convey fashions – *les grands couriers de la mode* – have also had a long history. They were made for several centuries before the bisque-head lady dolls that were made in the late 19th century. But before looking at the history of fashion dolls in general, it is necessary to explain why these beautiful dolls are called fashion dolls.

Defining the Name of the Doll

The use of the term "fashion doll" to describe the bisque-head doll produced between 1860 and 1890, has been the cause of extensive argument in the ranks of enthusiasts. The purists argue that the term is incorrect in that the phrase can apply only to the manner in which a doll is dressed – that is, in a fashionable way and contemporary with the period of the doll. If that is so, any doll, apart from baby dolls and *bébés*, may be dressed in this way and qualify as a fashion doll. This is unacceptable – at least to the purist.

Two other terms have been used to describe these bisque-head dolls. The term *Parisienne* found favour in 1885, when Jumeau produced a doll with a bisque head on a leather body that had the proportions of an adult female and called it *Poupée Parisienne*. Unfortunately, certain other French manufacturers, taking advantage of the weakness of national patent laws and trademark regulations, used the same name to describe other dolls of an entirely different type.

Another phrase that has been used, "lady doll," has the advantage of conveying an acceptable description of the body, similar to that produced by Jumeau, but gives no indication of the doll's prime asset – the gowns and dresses without which its major attraction would be greatly diminished.

Over the years there has been much debate about the words and terms used to describe the French bisque-head dolls, and it is to the credit of the United Federation of Doll Clubs that, in 1975, it decided to make a determined attempt to resolve the problem. Recognizing that authoritarian decisions based on the deliberations of a small, select committee might not meet with the approval of the mass of collectors, it adopted the more democratic method of inviting thousands of those concerned to participate by returning questionnaires on the subject. As a result it was decided to accept the phrase "fashion-type doll" to describe this particular doll, and to include the phrase in the official Glossary that was subsequently published. Undoubtedly it was a compromise, but one that, in view of all the circumstances, was easy to understand.

One would have expected that, with the passage of time, one name from all those available would have emerged to become universally accepted. But this has not happened. Today we find that there are supporters for all the candidates – fashion-type doll, lady doll, *Parisienne*, fashion doll – and there has even been a recent suggestion that the name "fashionable doll" should be used.

The expression fashion-type doll was the preference of the U.F.D.C. Lady doll is really better suited to describing the undressed doll. *Parisienne* has the romantic attraction of the doll's French ancestry. So what can be said about the last serious contender, fashion doll? The simple answer is that, in recent times, it has established itself as the most popular term, and it is therefore more used than

An unmarked, Bru-type doll, with blue glass eyes and moulded ears. This doll, which has a bisque head and swivel neck, and a leather body, is also illustrated on pages 74–5.

any of the others. It is used by a majority of dealers and collectors; it appears in doll magazines and auction details. The purist might object, but common usage makes it impossible to ignore, and it is, therefore, the name used in this book.

The Origins of the French Fashion Doll

A great deal has been written about the history of fashion dolls, and there has, in particular, been much speculation about their original purpose. Were they intended as children's playthings, or did they have the more mundane and commercial purpose of providing fashion designers and dressmakers with a convenient way of displaying their wares?

It is undeniable that records dating from the early 14th century show that samples of the latest fashions, suitably displayed on lifelike figures, were sent to other regions and other countries as three-dimensional fashion plates. But this practice of sending fully dressed figures as fashion samples, although lasting until the late 18th century, was mainly confined to an interchange of ideas between the royal courts of Europe, as only royalty and the noble families who supported them were rich enough to indulge in such luxuries.

The figures on which such gowns were displayed were neither toys nor dolls, both of which are, by definition, playthings for children. These figures most certainly did not come into this category. They may, after they had served their original purpose, have been given to a child to play with, but this changes nothing. Children have always been happy to incorporate adult items into their daily activities, and this does not make the items, *per se*, toys. Some importance has been attached to the fact that the word "doll" was used in the Middle Ages to refer to early fashion figures, but this might have been because there was no other suitable word in medieval times or because the records were incorrectly translated.

The correct term for this fashion figure is mannikin (or manikin), which derives from the Dutch, *manneken*. The earliest samples, first recorded in 1396, were made of carved wood and were quite large, sometimes almost life-size. Carved wooden figures still exist that might have been used for this purpose, but it has not proved possible to establish beyond all doubt that fashion display was their original purpose as the gowns have long vanished and there is insufficient other evidence to allow a positive judgement to be made. Further confusion may have arisen from the existence of fully articulated wooden figures used by artists to simulate the human form. These have been used for centuries and are still produced.

An example of a doll being used as a means of conveying fashions may have occurred as early as 1301, when Phillip IV of France sent a figure, complete with wardrobe, to his daughter, Isabella, who was about to marry the future Edward II of England. As Isabella was then only eleven years of age, we cannot be sure if the present was meant as a guide to fashions or simply as a pretty plaything. Possibly the ladies of the court saw it as the former and the future queen as the latter.

It is worth mentioning two other occasions when similar gifts were despatched from French courts. In 1496 Anne of Brittany, Queen of France, sent examples of the latest fashions to the Spanish queen, Isabella. Isabella was far from impressed and returned them to France, where the doll was promptly re-dressed and dispatched, at great speed, via the next pack-horse train to Spain. In 1600, Henry IV of France sent his betrothed, Marie de Medici, samples of the styles current at the French Court.

By the 17th century the use of a mannikin figure to convey latest fashions to the various courts of Europe had become more common. But the pract-

ice reached the heights of its popularity during the following century, when the establishment of many small states, each with a self-generating aristocracy enriched by the increased opportunities for travel and the free passage of goods, provided greater scope for the purveyors of fashion to promote their wares. The French fashion houses were the main beneficiaries, and they were not slow to build on their success.

The English were not backward in showing an interest in the importation of feminine styles, and regular supplies of dressed mannikins began to flow across the English Channel. This traffic was threatened by the war of the Spanish Succession (1701–14), when England and her allies fought France, Spain, Bavaria and Portugal. The free movement of most trade goods ceased, but such was the power and determination of the ladies that fashion mannikins were expressly excluded from this embargo and continued to circulate among the

various combatant countries – a wonderful example of "the Power of the Petticoat."

In 1780 Marie-Antoinette, wife of Louis XVI of France, sent several figures dressed in the latest fashions to her mother, Maria Theresa, Archduchess of Austria, and her sisters at the Austrian court. These figures had been attired by Rose Bertin, dressmaker to the royal court. Rose Bertin left a description of one of these figures: "a big doll with springs; a well-made foot and a very good wig. A fine linen chemise; a long well-boned corset." There is also a list of the figure's wardrobe, which included ball gowns and other dresses. When the French Revolution erupted, Rose, together with such aristocrats as were able to escape, emigrated to England, but poor Marie-Antoinette was less fortunate and lost both her crown and her head.

In spite of the use of the word "doll" in Rose Bertin's description, it is clear that the figure in question was a mannikin, and that it was most probably life-size. Figures up to 36in (90cm) tall and intended for similar use are generally referred to as *pandoras*. They are sometimes found with head, torso and arms, but with no legs, merely a slat support from waist to ground. *Pandoras* appear to have been first mentioned in 1642, and both they and the life-size mannikins continued to be used throughout the 17th and 18th centuries to convey the latest fashions.

It is known that in their efforts to promote the sale of their products, Paris fashion houses in the 18th century sent many dressed figures to America, and journals in that country carried advertisements offering a whole range of the latest fashions created in Europe. It is interesting to note that, almost without exception, the word used to describe the figures on which the dresses were displayed was "mannikin." This can only support the theory that the occasional use of the term "doll" was simply carelessness.

But the days of the mannikin were numbered. The beginning of the Industrial Revolution in the 18th century and more widely available education led to higher standards of literacy in general and, in particular, an increase in the demand for journals, magazines and books. The newly created middle classes provided a market for those luxury items that had previously been accessible only to the aristocratic classes. New-found wealth quickly led to a desire by the ladies of these households to display all the outward signs of their new position on the social scale, and the business of *haute couture* rapidly responded with creations that culminated in the fantastic examples of the following century.

Various means were used to spread the news that "clothes maketh the man," or, in this case, the woman, and full use was made of the printing industry, both by word and illustration. Fashion magazines appearing during the 18th century often featured hand-coloured illustrations.

The eminent Parisian doll making firm of Jumeau, which was manufacturing dolls between 1842 and 1899, was a great believer in the power of promotion and advertising and seldom missed an opportunity to extend the market for its products. The main targets for its advertisements were the young daughters of the richer families, and the company must have been well aware of this when it advertised its "fashion models." Not only could these young girls now have dolls dressed in the height of fashion, they could also obtain new models at regular intervals, and if they could not have a fully dressed doll then at least they could have another gown in the latest style – and all from the house of Jumeau!

It is now known that Jumeau exported fashion dolls to England, Spain and Germany, advertising them as "fashion models" dressed in the very latest *haute couture* gowns. This has led some people to suggest that these particular Jumeau dolls had the primary purpose of being conveyors of fashion, but this is highly unlikely.

Another way in which the latest fashions could be displayed was by the paper dolls, which were first produced in England during the last quarter of the 18th century. Originally intended as a simple toy for children, different dresses could be cut out and superimposed on the picture of the doll. But the French were quick to see the commercial possibilities of these dolls as a way to advertise the latest Paris fashions. Prospective customers could be supplied with this novel form of sales catalogue, which illustrated the prevailing trends and at the same time entertained the young members of the family.

This stimulation of interest in fashions added fresh impetus to the need to improve and increase the production of printed material, and, by 1830, at least six fully illustrated fashion magazines were being published in Paris, with more appearing as the years passed. These magazines not only greatly boosted the fashion trade, but they also sounded the deathknell for the life-size mannikin as a trade accessory.

By 1860 Charles Worth, an expatriate Englishman working in Paris, had promoted the use of live models to display his creations, and this practice was quickly adopted by other major fashion houses. (It is rather sad that the females so employed were termed "mannequins," as the meaning of this word at that time was "a dressmaker's dummy or lay figure.")

The arrival of the fashion house, where ladies could inspect at their leisure the latest creations of an increasingly powerful industry, coincided with vast improvements in transportation, which meant that the rich, even from distant places, could visit Paris and other centres of *haute couture* with comparative ease. Their less fortunate sisters, just as eager to be kept informed of the latest modes and trends, relied on the regular issue of fashion papers and magazines.

It is remarkable that, at a time of growing literacy and the publication of increasing numbers of fashion journals, the years between 1860 and 1890 saw the famous makers of the French bisque-head fashion dolls producing many of the finest examples of this particular doll. Only at the end of the century did the quantity and quality of these dolls decline.

The impetus toward the manufacture of fashion dolls came with the development of the process of manufacturing bisque *c.*1850. This twice-fired, but unglazed, porcelain, which could be delicately tinted and coloured between firings, lent itself perfectly to the production of lady-like dolls' heads with natural colours. Although they did not immediately or entirely replace glazed china or even papier mâché heads, bisque-head dolls became so popular that their manufacture in Paris developed into an important industry very quickly.

It is thought that the smaller bisque-head dolls were made as toys, which would have had the additional purpose of helping to educate girls and young women in the domestic skills they would require in later life. Larger examples, some over 30in (76cm), however, are more likely to have been occasionally used to promote and advertise the latest fashions.

Western culture has traditionally held that a woman's place is in the home, tending to the needs of husband and children. This might well have been an admirable ideal, but, at the time with which we are concerned, the number of women greatly exceeded that of men, and women had to face an unpalatable truth: outside marriage their choice was both limited and demeaning. Factories were beginning to replace agriculture as the main employers, but the hours were long and the pay miserly. Some larger households offered a variety of jobs under similar terms and conditions. For at least one daughter in each family there was the frightening prospect of having to take care of ageing parents until all hope of marriage and independence was gone. These truths brought great pressure to bear on young girls to make every effort possible to assure themselves of a good position in the race for matrimony. How could this be done?

Charm and beauty alone were not enough. If the aspiring bride was to be assured of her future, she could not afford to neglect any opportunity to shine in her social circle, and her outward appearance, which could be enhanced by a knowledge of fashion and the wearing of suitable gowns and accessories, was a crucial element in her success or otherwise.

In the 19th century extremely young girls produced wonderful examples of their needlework in samplers, many of which still exist. Completing these was not some form of occupational therapy; the samplers were intended to demonstrate skills that might later help these girls to find employment in those areas where they would be appreciated, including the homes of upper-class families. The more pampered daughters of upper-class families would be acquiring similar skills, but for more ambitious reasons – in preparation for their entry into the marriage market.

Any type of doll can be used for this purpose and undoubtedly is, but the shape of the fashion dolls' body provided the chance for children to dress dolls in exact replicas of adult fashions, something that the mannikin, not being a toy, had never done. This must surely go part of the way to explaining why many beautiful examples of the fashion doll were produced and purchased during the second half of the 19th century.

The original purpose of this particular doll might well have been as another plaything to entertain childlike hands and minds, but perhaps it was no coincidence that the dolls began to gain in popularity at precisely that time when women were intensely involved in the rigorous dictates of style and fashion. In this atmosphere it was hardly surprising that a daughter's toy also served as a means to awaken her interest and educate her in one of the most important of the social graces. Assisted by the many women who composed the normal household of those times, and using the abundant supply of materials then available, she could design, cut, sew and produce exquisite copies of the fashionable gowns worn by her mother. Many toys of that period had an educational aspect, but the fashion doll must have had a very important place. It seems fair to assume that this educational aspect might often have been a positive factor in any decision to present a young girl with this particular doll.

French Fashion Dolls and the German Challenge

French workshops were the first in Europe to produce bisque dolls' heads on a wide scale, and firms large and small were established to meet the new demand. The identity of most of the smaller doll makers is now known, and extensive research, much of it carried out by experts in the United States, has left few gaps in the knowledge about the major manufacturers. But there are still doubts about the extent of the "cross-trading" that occurred between the various sectors of the trade.

Jumeau opened a new factory at Montreuil-sous-Bois near Paris in 1873. An official report published later that year stated that "the factory [at Montreuil] is making doll heads of great perfection and has surpassed in beauty the products previously bought from Saxony [Germany]. He [Jumeau] has freed us from our former obligation to have foreigners furnish us with porcelain doll heads."

The implications of that last sentence are interesting. It suggests that Jumeau had previously been compelled to buy in some of the items needed to assemble complete dolls. It has even been suggested that, before 1873, Jumeau had not produced heads of bisque but only of glazed china. If true, this would indicate that any bisque heads must have come from another source, possibly Saxony.

Many other French doll makers and doll dealers conducted their business on a similar basis, and the smallest – of which there were hundreds – undoubtedly purchased on a large scale from outside sources. The bodies would have been well within their capacity to produce, but the equipment, skill and expense required to produce bisque heads, and

It is believed that the first glass eyes made especially for dolls were produced in England, but the French and German manufacturers perfected the technique. By the end of the 19th century about three-quarters of these eyes were made in Germany, but it was the French who produced the most beautiful and highly praised examples – the paperweight eyes, so called because they resembled glass paperweights in their appearance of depth.

There are many accounts of what was involved in producing these eyes, but unfortunately, most were written by journalists, who were more concerned with dramatic incidents than technical details. There can be no doubt, however, that it was an exacting craft. A novice eye maker would produce eyes for a year or more before worthwhile examples were made. Until that time, much of what was produced would be used only in cheaper dolls.

It was essential that an eye maker had perfect vision and a steady hand, which helps to explain why the craft was conducted almost entirely by young women, who had the necessary physical attributes; they were also cheaper to employ.

Some reports state that the work was undertaken in complete darkness. Although no definite reasons for this are given, it is reasonable to assume that the darkness allowed the eye maker to concentrate totally on the focal point of her work, with the only source of light provided by the brilliant gas jet. The eyestrain resulting from working in such conditions may only be imagined.

An eye maker used coloured glass rods of various thicknesses and a gas jet in which they could be heated and manipulated. The intensity of heat generated by the jet could be varied by changing the proportions of gas and air, and, as the eye maker needed to have both hands free, the controls for the gas jet were often operated by foot pedals.

Using a tube of white, opaque glass, the eye maker would first blow an eyeball to the required size. Then, taking a narrow rod of coloured glass, usually blue or brown but occasionally violet or hazel, she would heat the glass to melting point and lay a circle on the surface of the eyeball to represent the

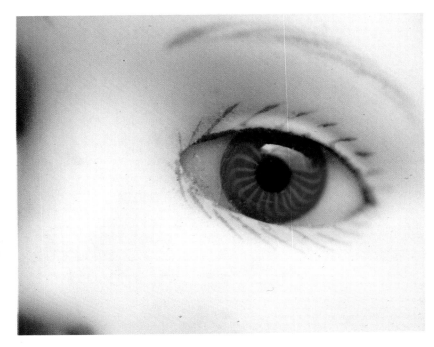

iris. Another glass rod, usually black, would then be heated and applied to the centre of the iris to form the pupil, while a further fine line of this, or another suitable colour, would be laid around the outside circumference of the iris.

The final stages required the greatest skill of all. An extremely fine rod of white glass was drawn out in the flame and laid in many minute lines between the pupil and the outer edge of the iris to give the eye a more life-like look. Finally, the pupil and iris were sometimes covered by a layer of molten crystal glass, which further enhanced the appearance of the eye.

There were, of course, many variations on the above methods, and the main part of a "fixed" eye was often produced by pouring molten glass into a mould. Even then, however, the coloured glass was applied in the way described above.

A skilled eye maker could produce wonderful examples, but however experienced and talented, it was almost impossible for an eye maker to produce perfectly matching pairs to order. Therefore, many eyes had to be sorted and examined to find the best possible match. Some eyes had minute cracks,

which appeared during the annealing (heating and cooling) process, but, at the time, these were not considered of sufficient importance to prevent their use. Many of today's collectors have overlooked this and have assumed that slightly mis-matched eyes are positive proof that one or the other eye is a recent replacement and that any other eye imperfection has resulted from subsequent mis-handling. It is sad that these incorrect assumptions have occasionally led to the replacement of original eyes.

The eye illustrated above is from a doll that has a Simonne stamp on its chest. The doll has bisque arms, a leather body with gussets at hips and knees, and a swivel neck.

the professional painting involved, must have made the attractions of buying-in hard to resist.

The house of Jumeau, among others, must have benefited from this situation. The Paris Chamber of Commerce directory of 1881 records that the firm were "suppliers to leading Paris novelty shops and specialists in making porcelain heads." And the fact that Jumeau-type heads have been found on bodies made by Lacmann, who had a doll business in Cincinnati, U.S.A., does not entirely preclude the possibility that Jumeau exported unfinished heads to the United States.

However, it is now believed that a considerable number of French dolls displayed heads manufactured in Germany. This is in spite of the fact that the French led the world in the large-scale production of fine dolls and that, apart from a home market hungry for the products of the many factories in and around Paris, it was the French to whom the rest of Europe and America looked for a continuing supply of dolls of all types. It is possible the sheer pressure of this demand finally undermined the dominance of the French in the doll making industry.

Like many other manufacturers of glazed china- and bisque-head dolls, two of the major names in the German sector, Simon & Halbig and Armand Marseille, started life as manufacturers of porcelain, and both established factories c.1865 – Armand Marseille at Köppelsdorf and Simon & Halbig at Grafenhain. Not until 1892, however, do German records mention Armand Marseille as making porcelain dolls' heads. If, as is almost certainly the case, the firm had been producing such heads before that time, it would mainly have been as sub-contractors to the trade. But no progressive manufacturing company is ever content to rely forever on this form of business, especially if it can see that the demand for its finished product is increasing internationally.

When the major German doll manufacturers entered the market in the 1880s they did so with typical German organization and thoroughness. Large factories were soon in production, and their output soon became a torrent. The first result of this was only to be expected: the new exports undercut the prices of longer established manufacturers.

For a considerable time the French, with their long experience in the industry and the superior quality of their product, were able to cope with the competition. But by the end of the century, German manufacturers directly threatened the future prosperity of the major French companies, a number of which decided to form a consortium to both produce and market their dolls. This was the Société Française de Fabrication de Bébés et Jouets (S.F.B.J.) and, in a way, it presaged the end of French dominance of the industry. Falling prices and profits led to a noticeable drop in the quality of dolls, and the work of firms such as Jumeau and Bru suffered accordingly. Perhaps this might have been their fate from the start, but the intervention of German competition certainly hastened the end.

Fortunately, the French fashion doll, as distinct from French dolls in general, proved more successful in resisting the pressure of foreign competition. *Haute couture*, an essential part of the overall attraction of the doll, was a predominantly French talent, and this factor alone prevented German competitors from making any real progress in this area.

The French Fashion Dolls' Wardrobe

Both the manufacturers and retailers of fashion dolls were always prepared to supply the dolls with or without their clothes, and, as a miniature reproduction of an exotic gown might well have cost more than the doll, it is easy to understand why the undressed version was popular. A number of undressed dolls might well have been dressed by the *haute couture* industry to the order of a wealthy client as a present for an over-indulged daughter, but most would have been entrusted to one or another of the females at the child's home where, with the dressmaking skills that were then commonplace, it could be suitably attired. Of course, if the child were old enough, she would have been given sole responsibility for the work involved as part of her education.

Dressed dolls usually reflected the very latest in Parisian fashions, including the multiple undergarments that were a feature of the period (see pages 138–9). And no self-respecting doll would consider her wardrobe complete without some of the multitude of accessories that were then available – hats, gloves, purses and bags, fans, muffs, even an occasional lorgnette or chatelaine. Moreover, miniature trunks containing these and other items could be bought for the doll, and today these are highly prized collectors' items. Many dolls do not themselves fit inside their original trunks, since, at the time they were bought, the trunks were intended only to contain the dolls' accessories.

Because a fashion doll would generally have been dressed in the height of current fashion, it might seem that a straightforward way of dating the doll itself would be to date the dress. But the reality is not so simple. Only if a complete and documented history of the doll exists, from the time it was placed into the hands of its first owner, can we be sure that the dress is "original." Surprisingly, such examples do exist, supported not only by written records but sometimes even by photographic evidence. But whether a dress is "all original" is often impossible to establish unequivocally, and the fact that the doll itself could be over one hundred and twenty-five years old compounds the difficulty. It is possible that, during the second half of the 19th century, when fashions changed with great rapidity, the doll might have been dressed and re-dressed by the original owner, handed on to a daughter or granddaughter and subjected to an updating of costume at their hands. Some of the beautiful gowns found on these dolls might well have been made thirty or more years after the doll itself. The phrase "original to the period" is, therefore, used to describe dresses that closely approximate to the age of the doll but for which no firm records exist.

In trying to establish the age of a dress and whether this matches the period of the doll, it is only possible, in the absence of documentary evidence, to examine the visual evidence. Does *all* the material used appear to be genuinely antique and such as would be obtainable at the time? Does it show signs of normal ageing? It should be remembered that such dresses would have been constantly arranged and rearranged by little fingers, and, even if physical handling had been kept to a minimum, over-exposure to strong sunlight or protracted storage in drawers or cupboards would have caused the fabric to deteriorate. In addition, in previous times an original dress, on becoming soiled, would have been quickly discarded in favour of a new outfit. Fortunately, more knowledgeable collectors nowadays happily accept some signs of wear and tear, provided that the garment is a genuine period costume. Such a dress would have to be almost disintegrating before the doll could be re-dressed with a clear conscience.

It is a common fallacy that dresses from this period must all have been made with fine hand stitching. The sewing machine came into more common use during the second half of the 19th century, and parts of even quite expensive gowns show signs of machine stitching. Of course, handwork is more common and ranges from comparatively large running stitches to exquisitely fine stitches that can be examined properly only with a magnifying glass. Cheaper dresses and those produced by children show the greatest use of the running stitch, while those made by the professional seamstresses incorporated a variety of stitches. Even the underclothes were often ornately decorated with lace, embroidery and fine stitching.

Between 1860 and 1890 many of the cheaper gowns were factory produced and simple in presentation, with cotton, butter muslin, organdie and nun's veiling (a fine wool), being the most common fabrics in use. More silk, satin and lace, together with artificial flowers, miniature jewellery and other embellishments were used in the more exotic items produced by professional seamstresses.

When it has been established that the clothes have the physical appearance that suggests that they could be a century or more old, it is necessary to compare the style of the gown with the age of the doll itself. If the age of the doll can be determined with any certainty, we would expect that the fashion of the gown it wears, if completely original, would correspond with that period. Since 19th-century fashions were generally very exaggerated and changed in comparatively short periods, if the fashion period does not correspond with the age of the doll, it is fairly certain that the dress is from a different period from the time the doll was first dressed, and that it is not original to the doll.

In the final analysis it is almost impossible to set out completely infallible guidelines for the instant recognition of a truly original gown, but the factors already mentioned, together with constant and continuing examination of all available examples, will finally lead to that indefinable ability to judge and assess the authenticity and quality of a fashion doll.

Dressed for a pleasant morning cutting flowers, the doll on the left wears a striped cotton dress, a late 19th-century version of the type of dress worn by young girls in the 1830s, with brace-like trimming, full puffed sleeves and a gathered skirt with a bow at the waist. The matching bib-apron is trimmed with zig-zag braid. The silk hat dates from the 1900s as does the fan, which is made from an ivory-like composition and painted with forget-me-knots.

The doll on the right is in a morning dress of c.1868 made from printed cotton trimmed with eyelet embroidery. Her outfit consists of a semi-fitted jacket, which is draped up at the back with internal tapes. The matching skirt is fuller at the back, where it is tightly pleated and supported with a collapsible wire bustle belonging to the 1880s. The hat is of silver-grey straw braid and has a wide turned-up brim, trimmed with lace and forget-me-knots.

Lying across the flower basket is a parasol of the 1860s to 1870s with a turned ivory handle. The loop at the ferrule end enabled it to be held upside down in a closed position. The late 19th-century gloves are of knitted silk.

LEFT-HAND DOLL
MARKS Incised *B.S.* on shoulder-plate. SIZE 21½in (55cm). DATE *c.*1860. HEAD Swivel neck, blue glass eyes (resembles early Steiner). BODY All leather with gussets at elbows, hips and knees. BODY STYLE A3 (page 124).

RIGHT-HAND DOLL
MARKS Unmarked; attributed Jumeau. SIZE 21½in (55cm). HEAD Swivel neck; blue glass eyes. BODY All leather with gussets at elbows, hips and knees; separate stitched toes. BODY STYLE E1 (page 126).

FRENCH FASHION DOLLS 1860-90

The French fashion dolls illustrated in this book represent examples ranging from the better known to the very rare. These dolls are described in detail on the following pages, but it is also worthwhile recording details of a few other interesting types of fashion doll that are not shown as well as some of the major international collections where they may be seen.

The Margaret Woodbury Strong Museum, Rochester, New York, is a veritable goldmine for all those interested in children's playthings, and fashion dolls form an important part of the exhibits. (It is interesting that this section is displayed under the title of *Parisiennes*!) Of particular note are a marked Huret, with gutta-percha body and bisque hands, and a marked Rohmer, which has a bisque head and intaglio eyes on a jointed wood body with swivel waist and metal hands. There is also an excellent Steiner, marked with an incised C, which has lever eyes and is mounted on a leather body. Steiner also produced lady dolls' bodies of "blown kid."

Also of interest are the two Rochard patent fashion dolls displayed in the museum and the copy of the patent papers, part of which is illustrated opposite. This *Brevet d'Invention*, dated Paris, 27 March 1867, is for a process by which miniature "jewels" in the form of a necklace could be inserted into the necks and shoulder-plates of dolls. The official record refers to a kaleidoscope, but not just pretty colours were involved – reproduced on the tiny surfaces of the jewels are wonderfully detailed scenes and figures of people, which can be viewed through a cavity cut in the rear of the shoulder-plate. (Another example of this doll is in the possession of Elsie Potter in England, and it is shown on pages 102–3. Inside the head is the signature *Rochard Breveté Déposé*.) The museum also has an interesting example of a Josef Kubelka type doll. This Austrian gentleman obtained in

1884 multinational patents for a process whereby wax was poured into a cavity at the top of the doll's head; hair could then be inserted into the wax.

The Gladys Hillsdorf Collection in the United States contained two very interesting marked Huret fashion dolls; it has been suggested that they were originally given as "table favours" to important guests who attended a Paris banquet in 1860. One of the dolls is incised "Marie de Provence" and the other "Denise de Bourgogne;" both these ladies were famous courtesans of the time. It could well be that these two "portrait dolls" formed part of a series that Huret is believed to have produced. Both dolls have bisque heads with straight-flange necks and brown-painted eyes, but while Marie has an all-wood, articulated body, Denise has a wood, articulated body with bisque hands. Another interesting fashion doll in this collection is marked *Bru Jne & Cie No 2*, and there are two fine examples of the Rochard patent doll.

The Museum of the City of New York contains a large range of antiques of all descriptions, but the department devoted to dolls and toys, although not as large as in some other museums, displays its contents with great artistry and imagination. It was here that the curator, John Noble, produced a most interesting piece of information: he had found, in another section of the museum, full-size, adult gowns from the house of Worth in Paris, while in the doll department are fashion dolls dressed in identical Worth fabrics. Both full-size and miniature gowns reflect the same style, and it seems most likely that the different sized gowns were manufactured at the same time. We cannot be certain how this came about – a present from Worth to the daughter of an important client? Made by the family from left-over material? Or did Worth supply unwanted material to a Parisian dressmaker who specialized in clothes for dolls?

The museum has far more items than can ever

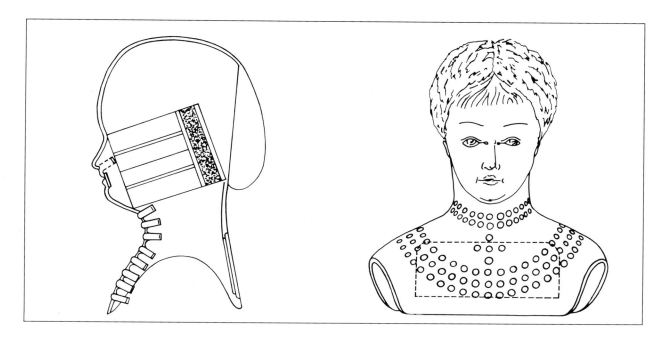

be displayed at the same time, so it is customary, every nine or twelve months, to change the exhibits around so that the returning visitor can always find a new display to delight him.

Technical information about each of the dolls illustrated – height, marks, body material and so on – is given at the foot of each relevant caption. Included in these details for each doll is a body-style code – M3, for example – which allows the dressed doll to be compared with one of the undressed dolls illustrated on pages 124–32. The body-style codes refer only to the dolls' bodies – material, gussets, joints and so forth; they do not refer to the dolls' heads, and the heads on the undressed dolls are not necessarily of the same style or type as the heads on dressed dolls, even though the body-style is identical.

The following points should also be borne in mind when the illustrations and captions are studied.

◇ The manufacturer of a doll is positively stated only when the doll is fully marked. The use of the word "attributed" when describing a doll indicates that, in every respect but size, the doll is identical to other, fully marked examples and is, in the author's opinion, the product of that manufacturer. The use of the word "type"

indicates that the doll closely resembles other, fully marked examples.

◇ The majority of the fashion dolls shown bear neither incised nor printed marks. Such marks did not become commonplace until near the end of the 19th century.

◇ Only exceptional circumstances allow the age of a doll to be precisely stated. The dolls illustrated were almost entirely produced between 1865 and 1885; a few might overlap that period by five years either way.

◇ The following types of body joints are referred to in the captions and may be seen in the illustrations of the undressed dolls. *Socket joint* is the term used to describe the joint created when the hemispherical end of one limb fits into the socket of another. When the joint is made by two flat surfaces lying against each other, sometimes with a retaining ridge, it is described as a *flange joint*. There are many variations in the style and type of *tenon joints*, but the term is here used to indicate those joints that more closely resemble a traditional mortise-and-tenon joint than any other.

◇ The mounting of dolls' heads takes one of three

21

forms. When a hemispherical neck fits into the socket of a shoulder-plate, allowing both side-to-side and up-and-down movement of the head, the mounting is described as a *swivel neck*. (This style is sometimes also called a swivel head.) The term *flange neck* is used to describe a flat-surface joint that allows only side-to-side movement of the head; it is an earlier version of the swivel neck mounting and was patented by Rohmer in 1858. When there is no joint between the head and shoulder-plate the mounting is described as a *fixed neck*. (This style is sometimes referred to as fixed head.) Although dolls with fixed necks are rarer than those with swivel necks, they are less popular with collectors. Huret is believed to have patented a swivel neck in 1861, but, possibly because it was cheaper to produce, the fixed type continued to be used after that date.

◇ With the exception of one china-head doll (glazed porcelain, see pages 106–7) and a bisque head mounted directly on to a metal body (see pages 94–5), all the dolls illustrated have heads and shoulders of bisque (unglazed porcelain).

◇ Many different materials were used to stuff the bodies of leather dolls, including horsehair, powdered cork and sawdust. Sawdust is by far the most common and also the heaviest.

The fashion dolls illustrated on the following pages are, unless otherwise indicated, those that have passed through the hands of the author during her many years as a dealer, lecturer and expert in antique dolls. Fashion expert Madeleine Ginsburg, of the Victoria & Albert Museum, London, has contributed the detailed descriptions of the garments illustrated as well as an appendix on 19th-century women's underwear (see pages 138–9).

These two dolls are dressed in sombre promenade gowns. The doll on the left has a dress with a gathered trimming of fringed black silk and faced with red, dating from c.1880. The long-waisted, fitted bodice is made from velvet, with ribbon bands trimming both the bodice and the decoratively gathered petticoat insert. The fullness of the skirt is pulled back into a gentle puff. Her velvet bonnet has a veil of embroidered net. She also has a walking length umbrella with an ivory and wood handle, metal ribs and a black cotton cover with a matching slip case. Pinned to her dress is a photographic miniature of the 1890s in a gilt case.

The other doll wears a velvet outfit faced with silk of 1868–70. Under the hip-length jacket, the tails of which are trimmed with buttons, is a sleeveless silk waistcoat with a bow at the back. Her blouse is of white cotton embroidered in white. The hat, which is of the same period, is made from straw and is trimmed with a silk bow and silk flowers. Her high-heeled shoes, made from black glacé kid, are low cut and trimmed with a silver rosette. A gilt metal sovereign purse, hooked on at the waist, contains miniature, mock "gold" coins.

LEFT-HAND DOLL
MARKS Unmarked; attributed Jumeau. SIZE 20in (51cm). HEAD Swivel neck; blue glass eyes; pierced ears. BODY All leather with gussets at elbows, hips and knees. BODY STYLE A1 (page 124).

RIGHT-HAND DOLL
MARKS Unmarked. SIZE 19in (48cm). HEAD Swivel neck; blue glass eyes; pierced ears. BODY Leather over wood with bisque forearms and lower legs; tenon joints at shoulders, elbows, hips and knees. BODY STYLE G3 (page 127). (*Jackie Jacobs*)

Appropriately dressed to exercise her dog, this lady is wearing a summer walking dress made from printed silk. Both her hat and dress are of an asymmetric design that Bru was fond of using. Her gown, which dates from c.1880, is trimmed with embroidered net. It consists of a diagonal-fastening, hip-length jacket bodice with ties at the hips, through which the train is looped. The skirt is walking length and is mounted on taffeta and trimmed at the hem with a double layer of frills. Her forward-tilted hat has a flat crown and a brim trimmed with a velvet band and streamers; it may be of an earlier date than the rest of her costume. The silk parasol has whalebone ribs. The flat-heeled boots are of red morocco and fasten at the sides. She carries a purse of the 1860s. It is rare to find a fashion doll dressed in printed silk.

MARKS Incised G on both head and shoulder-plate; attributed Bru. SIZE 19½in (50cm). HEAD Swivel neck; unusual glass eyes flecked with brown, green and blue; pierced ears. BODY All leather with gussets at elbows, hips and knees. BODY STYLE A3 (page 124).

This oriental doll, *which is a very rare example of this class, is wearing an informal summer outfit of c.1868 with the back interest that began to be fashionable in the later 1860s. It is made from white cotton with a ribbed finish, which is edged with woven, zig-zag braid, and it consists of a three-quarter length jacket, draped at the back of the hips, and with wide, flared sleeves. The matching skirt is flared at the front, pleated at the back and trimmed with a deep flounce at the hem. There are lace frills around the edge of the jacket. She wears only one of her gilt "ruby, diamond and emerald" pendant earrings and a gilt fob watch.*

The doll is standing in front of a mahogany screen, which is inlaid with mother-of-pearl. The red lacquer bureau partially obscures a leather and brassbound doll's trunk. The reproduction Chippendale chair is also shown on pages 52–3.

MARKS Incised *E.B.* on shoulder-plate; attributed E. Barrois.
SIZE 16in (41cm). HEAD Swivel neck; brown glass eyes; pierced ears. BODY All leather; gussets at elbows only.
BODY STYLE N1 (page 130).

The two black sedan-bearers and lady shown here are dressed in the Louis Seize (18th-century) style that was so popular in the 1880s. The coats of the sedan-bearers, or chair-men, were originally mouse brown, trimmed and faced with deep pink, now faded to the palest pink, satin. The lady wears a loose-pleated "sack" dress, with pleats from the shoulders, of cream silk with a ribbed weave trimmed with lace. She has a pearl necklace, and pearls are entwined in her powder-white curls. Her fan has a painted silk leaf with feather border and bone sticks.

The age and fragility of the costumes worn by all three dolls made it impossible to contemplate undressing them to search for manufacturers' marks. In addition, the lady could not be removed from the sedan chair without damaging the chair, so technical details are not available beyond the fact that she has a swivel neck and bisque forearms. However, the facial characteristics of all three dolls closely resemble those of dolls known to have been made by F. Gaultier.

The main structure of the chair is covered with velvet that matches the coats of the sedan-bearers. Deep-buttoned, pink silk lines the chair's interior and is also used on the exterior panels, which have been hand painted with floral designs. Although the original colours of the material have faded with time, the chair is in perfect condition. The glass in the windows of the chair is bevelled, and there is a small trapdoor in the base, concealing a box designed to contain chocolates.

This complete group of dolls and sedan chair was originally owned by a Duke of Bedford; it is now part of the author's collection.

THE SEDAN-BEARERS

MARKS See above. SIZE 13in (33cm). HEADS Swivel neck; "fired-in-bisque" colouring; brown glass eyes; pierced ears. BODIES All leather with no gussets; stitched fingers. BODY STYLE F1 in brown leather, but stitched fingers (page 126).

Standing before her gown, which is carefully displayed on a dress form, is a doll who still retains much of her complete outfit of c.1865. She is wearing a lightly boned corset and one of her two sets of underwear. This set consists of a chemise, open drawers and gored petticoat, made from lawn and trimmed with lace and insertion. The other set, with a higher necked, front-fastening chemise and a pleated frill to the petticoat, would have been for less formal wear. She also wears a crinoline petticoat to support the full skirts of her dresses. Made from white figured cotton, stiffened with five rows of cane, it has an elastic waistband and two elastic tapes at the back to control its shape.

On the stand is her ball gown, in the very latest fashion and, with its crenellated trimmings, very similar to one shown in an 1865 fashion plate. The overdress is made from silk with a ribbed weave, trimmed with piping and silk fringe, while the gored skirt is made from satin with a very stiff lining. She

also has a pair of low-cut evening shoes of white satin, trimmed with blue bows and cut steel buckles, and wrist-length white kid gloves with a single button. Her blue silk fan, painted with wild roses, has ivory sticks and a tassel trimmed with a gilt loop. Her jewellery is suitable for both day and evening wear. To accompany her ball dress she has a tiara and a pendant necklace of "diamonds and sapphires," while for her day dress she has a necklace of gilt set with "turquoise," the pendant trimmed with beads en suite *with those on her promenade dress.*

This doll, wearing a different gown, is also illustrated on pages 90–1.

MARKS Unmarked, but very rare mould.   SIZE 19in (48cm). DATE *c*.1865.   HEAD Swivel neck; cobalt blue glass eyes; pierced ears.   BODY Leather over wood with tenon joints at shoulders, elbows, hips and knees; bisque forearms; moulded bosom as in C3. This type of body sometimes also has arms as in C3. BODY STYLE O1 (page 131).

Although only about ten years separate the outfits worn by these dolls, the difference between them is marked. The doll on the left wears a promenade dress of c.1875 made from silk with a ribbed weave. It has a fitted jacket bodice, with back interest at the hip, while the skirt is puffed up under an apron drape, which gives it the smooth front introduced in 1875. She wears a straw hat and carries kid gloves with scalloped, wrist-length cuffs, which fasten with a single china button. Her mid-calf-length, side-button boots are of bronze kid and have high heels.

The doll on the right is wearing a morning dress of c.1865 made of fine wool trimmed with ribbon and lace. A streamer of ribbon hangs from the back neckline of her flared jacket, emphasizing the loose triangular silhouette fashionable at that time. Her full skirt is box pleated at both front and back and has a double box pleat at each side. She wears a hat

trimmed with silk lace and ribbon, and she carries
kid gloves with two metal buttons at the wrist. Her
braid-trimmed silk parasol, which has an ivory
handle and whalebone and brass fittings, is not visible.

LEFT-HAND DOLL
MARKS Unmarked (F.G. type). SIZE 18½in (47cm). HEAD Swivel
neck; grey glass eyes; pierced ears. BODY All leather with gussets
at hips and knees; wood arms with tenon joints at shoulders and
elbows; socket-joint wrists with flange joints in upper arms.
BODY STYLE O2 (page 131).

RIGHT-HAND DOLL
MARKS Unmarked; attributed Bru. SIZE 16½in (42cm).
HEAD Swivel neck; blue glass eyes with moulded lower-lids;
pierced ears. BODY All leather with gussets at elbows, hips and
knees; separate stitched toes. BODY STYLE A3 (page 124).

Two children and a lady are shown here, grouped around a bureau. The lady is wearing a satin dress of c.1880, which shows some of the features introduced by the aesthetic movement – a loose smocked neckline and double-puffed sleeves. Her skirt, with its bustle, its drapes and puffs at the hip and its gathers, is in the height of fashion. Not quite so up-to-date, however, is her small black hat, which is more characteristic of the early 1870s, as are her high-heeled, square-toed, side-button boots. Her gilt locket contains a lock of hair.

Seated at the lady's feet is a girl dressed in the style of c.1875. Her small, close-brimmed hat matches the trimming on her check silk dress, and her front-fastening jacket bodice, which is draped at the back, has a belt with a black velvet bow. The flared skirt is knee length. She wears lace-up ankle boots with sensible, flat heels.

Standing to the side of the bureau is a small girl wearing a silk dress of the mid-1860s. It has pinked and gathered frills and a lace-edged, hip-length trimming over a knee-length, box-pleated skirt. Her papier maché hat dates from the 1880s.

RIGHT-HAND DOLL
MARKS Unmarked (Jumeau type). SIZE 15in (38cm).
HEAD Swivel neck; blue glass eyes; pierced ears. BODY All leather with gussets at elbows, hips and knees. BODY STYLE A1 (page 124).

SEATED DOLL
MARKS Unmarked (Simonne type). SIZE 12in (30cm).
HEAD Swivel neck; cobalt blue glass eyes; pierced ears.
BODY Leather over wood with tenon joints at shoulders, elbows, hips and knees; bisque arms. BODY STYLE O1 (page 131).

LEFT-HAND DOLL
MARKS Jumeau Médaille d'Or. SIZE 11in (28cm). HEAD Swivel neck; blue glass, almond-shaped eyes; pierced ears. BODY All leather with gussets at elbows, hips and knees.
BODY STYLE A1 (page 124).

Seated together on a couch with their pet dog are a mother and daughter. The mother is wearing a mantle of the mid-1860s. Made from light woollen cloth, it has an embroidered design around the edge. Her skirt, however, is more typical of the style seen in the 1870s.

The child wears a summer outfit of the early 1860s made from check woven cotton trimmed with braid. It consists of a bolero jacket, a box-pleated skirt and a matching pork-pie hat and a reticule. This outfit would have been very fashionable, for short-waisted bolero jackets were introduced for adult wear only about 1862–3. The hat and dress are made of matching material. Printed inside the hat are the words Au Calife de Bagdad, Rebbilion. *Taken in conjunction with the shop label that is fixed to the doll's chest (see below), this provides seldom found evidence that the clothes are completely original.*

THE MOTHER
MARKS Blue Huret stamp on chest.   SIZE 18½in (47cm).
HEAD Swivel neck; painted blue eyes; pierced ears.   BODY Leather over gutta-percha; bisque forearms; socket joints at shoulders, elbows and knees; diagonal-flange hip joints.
BODY STYLE H1 (page 127).

THE DAUGHTER
MARKS Oval shop label on chest with the indistinct word *Rebbilion* on it (see above).   SIZE 13in (33cm).   HEAD Fixed neck; blue glass eyes; pierced ears. A Huret-type face.   BODY All leather with bisque arms; gussets at hips and knees.
BODY STYLE J2 (page 128).

This lady, shown here with a German character doll of American President William McKinley, is wearing a ball dress of the late 1870s, made from cotton-backed satin. The form-fitting, corset-like bodice and the trained skirt, tied back with bands of gathering, are trimmed with silk lace, flowers and pearls. The tight, hip-length bodice and the skirt, tied back so that the knees are hobbled and all fullness is thrown to the back, are the significant fashion features of the years between 1876 and the early 1880s.

MARKS Incised *F.G.* on shoulder-plate. SIZE 16in (41cm).
HEAD Swivel neck; blue glass eyes; pierced ears. BODY All leather with gussets at elbows, hips and knees. BODY STYLE A1 (page 124).

Admiring themselves in a mirror are two ladies in crinolines. The doll on the left wears a satin court or formal ball dress of 1865–8. The matching bodice and train are trimmed with gathers of embroidered net that match the tiers of frills on her petticoat, while ribbon bows trim the front of her bodice and artificial flowers one side of the borders of her train and "pearls" the other. Court dresses always had trains, the length of which was regulated according to the etiquette of the court. They were worn with a headdress of lace and feathers.

The doll on the right wears a taffeta walking dress of 1866–7, trimmed with applied braid and tassels. The jacket, which is fitted but has no waistseam, has a flared back, while the skirt is very full and gored and has wide pleats at each side and a double box pleat at the back. It is faced with buckram for extra stiffness. In the mid-1860s the line became smoother and the silhouette triangular rather than rounded. She carries a feather fan typical of the 1880s.

LEFT-HAND DOLL
MARKS Unmarked; attributed "smiling" Bru. SIZE 19in (48cm). DATE c.1865. HEAD Swivel neck; blue glass eyes; pierced ears. BODY All leather; gussets at hips and knees; Bru brevette-style bisque hands. BODY STYLE E3 (page 126).

RIGHT-HAND DOLL
MARKS Unmarked (Simonne-type face). SIZE 18½in (47cm). DATE c.1860. HEAD Swivel neck; cobalt blue eyes. BODY All wood; tenon joints at shoulders, elbows, wrists, hips and knees; flange joints at waist and mid-thigh. BODY STYLE P1 (page 131).

These rear views of three splendid promenade dresses illustrate the detail and delicacy of these miniature gowns. The doll on the left wears a promenade dress of c.1872 made from silk with a ribbed weave. The collar, the deep, turned-back cuffs, the trimming at the back of the jacket and the two-tier skirt are faced with satin bands, and the jacket bodice fastens with satin-covered buttons, which continue down the centre of the overskirt. The jacket bodice is additionally trimmed with black and white lace, while the dress is given the back fullness fashionable in the 1870s by being supported on a substantial, square, straw-trimmed bustle. She has a straw sailor hat, with upturned brim, and carries a figured silk parasol. Her bronze kid, side-button boots, which have the mark c.c. and the size 2 impressed into the sole, have high heels.

The doll on the right wears a promenade dress of c.1868. It consists of a light wool overdress with bands over the shoulder, an apron front and a trained silk underdress, trimmed with braid and lace. She carries a netted bead bag with gilt mounts and a silk parasol. Her matching hat is elaborately trimmed with flowers and feathers. She wears low-cut black patent slippers with flat heels.

In the centre is a young girl wearing a silk dress of c.1885. It is fairly full and gathered at the yoke and low waistline, and it has a "Toby dog" frill of lace at the neck and lace frills on the cuffs and hem. Her straw hat, with its high-peaked brim, is trimmed with feathers, ribbon and flowers. She wears bronze kid, side-button boots with high heels; impressed on the sole is the size 2. This doll is also illustrated on pages 56–7.

LEFT-HAND DOLL
MARKS Unmarked (Simonne type). SIZE 15in (38cm). HEAD Swivel neck; cobalt blue eyes; pierced ears. BODY All leather with bisque arms; tenon joints at shoulders; gussets at hips and knees. BODY STYLE J3 (page 128).

RIGHT-HAND DOLL
MARKS Incised E on back of head and shoulder; attributed Bru. SIZE 16in (41cm). HEAD Swivel neck; blue glass eyes; pierced ears. BODY Cloth with leather arms; no gussets. BODY STYLE A2 (page 124).

CENTRE DOLL
MARKS Unmarked. SIZE 12in (30cm). HEAD Fixed neck; blue glass eyes; pierced ears. BODY All leather with gussets at elbows, hips and knees. BODY STYLE A1 (page 124).

Perhaps preparing to exercise her pet greyhound, the doll on the left wears a promenade dress of c.1875 of fine striped wool with gathered and machine-pleated trimming. Although the bustle remains, the style of the skirt is beginning to change, becoming flatter in front. The long-waisted jacket has pleated tails, and the skirt has tapes inside the train to hold the shape. Her wide-brimmed, 17th-century-style hat is trimmed with feathers and ribbon loops, and she carries a fur muff of approximately the same date.

The doll on the right wears a tightly fitting princess-line dress of c.1878, made from satin and once shell-pink in colour. The gathered drape at the hips and the pleated skirt are trimmed with striped satin and lace, and they illustrate the long-waisted, tightly draped style that was characteristic of the period. Her hat is of straw trimmed with ribbon and flowers. Her high-heeled, side-button boots are of bronze kid and have L. D. Déposé and 4 impressed on the sole.

LEFT-HAND DOLL
MARKS Incised *G* on head and shoulders; attributed "smiling" Bru.   SIZE 17in (43cm).   HEAD Swivel neck; blue glass eyes; pierced ears.   BODY All wood; tenon joints at shoulders, elbows, wrists, hips, knees and ankles; socket-joint swivel waist.
BODY STYLE E2 (page 126).

RIGHT-HAND DOLL
MARKS Incised *F.G.* on shoulder-plate and 4 on back of head and shoulder.   SIZE 18½in (47cm).   HEAD Swivel neck; blue glass eyes; pierced ears.   BODY All wood; tenon joints at shoulders, elbows, hips and knees; socket joints at wrists; flange joints at mid-upper arm and mid-thigh.   BODY STYLE P3 (page 131).

Posed between two jardinières are a mother and daughter. The mother wears a square-necked promenade dress, which fastens in the front. The gored and trained skirt is tightly gathered at the centre back and trimmed at the hem with box-pleated flounces. It has a sash with two wide pendant ends and a matching cape. The gown is made from taffeta, and the fringe is applied in the angular arrangement that was fashionable in 1867–8. The en suite bonnet is made from pleated paper and trimmed with pale blue ribbon and tulle. Her wig is in its original style and very fashionable, dressed high at the front, three rolls at the back (kept in place with a hair net) and two dangling "follow-me-lad" ringlets. Her pale blue leather boots have flat heels and a front lacing. She carries a fan with bone sticks and painted silk leaves, of the same date as the dress.

The girl, dressed in the style of c.1880, wears a silk-trimmed, fitted poplin coat, which has no waistseam. Trimmed with rows of pleats from hips to hem and fastened with pearl buttons, the coat is lined with cotton and has a lace frill at the hem. Her en suite hat is of straw trimmed with blue silk and decorated with steel buckles. Her bronze kid boots are buttoned at the side and have high heels, and she is wearing open-work cotton socks. In general, a girl's dress would have a similar line to an adult's, although it would be much shorter and omit the bustle.

THE MOTHER
MARKS Unmarked (Simonne type). SIZE 18in (46cm). HEAD Swivel neck; cobalt blue glass eyes. BODY Leather over wood with tenon joints at shoulders, elbows, hips and knees; bisque forearms. BODY STYLE O1 (page 131).

THE DAUGHTER
MARKS Unmarked (F.G. type). SIZE 15in (38cm). HEAD Swivel neck; blue glass eyes; pierced ears. BODY All leather with gussets at elbows, hips and knees. BODY STYLE A1 (page 124).

Standing with her two daughters, the mother in this group wears a matching four-piece outfit of c.1871, made from silk with a ribbed weave. She is dressed for outdoors in a sleeveless mantle, trimmed at the back with a bow, over a low-necked, tightly fitting bodice. Frilly trimming of the type on this dress was very fashionable in the early 1870s, and a fashion plate of 1871 shows a similar style to this. Her bone fan with its applied gilt flowers and her ivory opera glasses are of the same date. She also wears a curly brimmed, high-crowned hat, suede gloves with a button at the wrist and high-heeled, front-fastening bronze kid boots. Her outfit also includes a tangerine silk parasol with whalebone ribs, a brass ferrule and an ivory handle with an "amber" knob.

The daughter standing on the left of the group is dressed in a taffeta overdress with a draped and gathered back of 1868–9. Originally, the bright purple of the dress, which was a very popular colour at this period, would have contrasted vividly with the colours of the wound silk buttons, the braid and the silk lace of the trimming. The underdress is flared, mounted on buckram for extra stiffness and trimmed with pink frills. The glacé kid boots have flat heels and are trimmed at the toe with gilt buckles; the soles are impressed with the marks CC and 2.

The daughter in the centre wears a satin striped, ribbed silk overdress trimmed with applied braid. It has a flared skirt with a pointed border and a matching flared hip-length drape mounted over a cream wool underdress lined with glazed cotton for extra stiffness. The line is slightly straighter than that of her "sister's" purple dress, suggesting that it dates from a year or so earlier. She wears bronze kid, elastic-sided boots with high heels. The soles are impressed with the figure 2.

THE MOTHER
MARKS Unmarked. SIZE 17in (43cm). DATE *c.*1870. HEAD Swivel neck; cobalt blue glass eyes; pierced ears. BODY All leather with gussets at elbows, hips and knees. BODY STYLE A1 (page 124).

LEFT-HAND DOLL
MARKS Unmarked (Jumeau type). SIZE 14in (36cm).
DATE *c.*1865. HEAD Swivel neck; blue glass eyes; pierced ears.
BODY All leather with bisque arms; gussets at hips.
BODY STYLE M1 (page 130).

CENTRE DOLL
MARKS Unmarked (Simonne type). SIZE 15in (38cm).
DATE *c.*1865. HEAD Swivel neck; cobalt blue eyes; pierced ears.
BODY All leather with gussets at hips. BODY STYLE N3 but no elbow gussets (page 130).

49

Dressed for a shopping expedition, two ladies and a child, accompanied by their dogs, stand outside a shop. The doll on the left wears a light wool dress of c.1868, faced with tucks and trimmed with satin. The style – short-waisted and with sleeves flared and just below elbow length, the hem faced with buckram to give it extra swing – looks back to the 1860s, but her skirt, which is gored, gathered at the centre back and has a curving overskirt, looks forward to the 1870s. The hat, probably of the same date, is made from straw and faced with satin.

The doll on the right wears a silk tweed walking dress of c.1880. Lined with buckram, it is trimmed with a row of brass buttons from neck to knees, while at the back there is a shaped panel of black silk with a hobble drape fastening asymmetrically with a silk bow. Back interest on the bodice was a fashion feature c.1880. The bonnet, which is part of the original outfit, is made from straw trimmed with ribbon and flowers and has fringed silk ties. She carries a parasol with whalebone ribs and a wooden handle of c.1860. Her bone fan is of about the same date.

The doll in the centre is dressed as a small girl in a knee-length, blue cloth, walking outfit trimmed with woollen cloth and lace. It is closely fitted but has no waistseam, and it has a pleated back panel to the skirt and a gathered pocket on the hip. The front of the coat is trimmed with two rows of white silk buttons, but it actually fastens with hooks and eyes. The forward-tilted, beehive shaped hat, made from straw and trimmed with figured ribbon and feathers, is part of the original outfit. Her mid-calf length, side-button boots have high heels. They are of bronze kid and have steel buckles at the toe; impressed on the sole are the marks ⚙ and J. This doll, which is also illustrated on pages 56–7, dates from c.1880.

LEFT-HAND DOLL
MARKS Incised *B.S.* on shoulder-plate; oval Simonne stamp on chest. (An example of a doll produced from parts supplied by two different manufacturers.)   SIZE 15in (38cm).   HEAD Swivel neck; blue glass eyes; pierced ears.   BODY All leather with bisque arms; gussets at hips and knees.   BODY STYLE J3 (page 128).

RIGHT-HAND DOLL
MARKS Incised *2* on shoulder-plate. (F.G. type).
SIZE 15½in (39cm).   HEAD Swivel neck; grey glass eyes; pierced ears.   BODY All leather with gussets at elbows and hips.
BODY STYLE N3 (page 130).

CENTRE DOLL
MARKS Unmarked (Jumeau type).   SIZE 9½in (24cm).
HEAD Swivel neck; pale blue glass eyes; pierced ears.   BODY All leather; no gussets.   BODY STYLE N2 (page 130).

The art nouveau screen is decorated in the style of
Walter Crane, and the cabinet is decorated with
Chinese motifs; the chair is reproduction
Chippendale. The doll on the left is wearing a
promenade dress of 1876–8, made from striped silk
with a closely fitting, corset-like bodice, fastening in
the front, and an apron overdress tied at the back
over the trained underdress. It is trimmed with a frill
down the centre front and has two pockets. Her
bronze kid boots have high heels and side-button
fastenings. The size 4 and the mark CC are
impressed in the sole. Her bone fan is somewhat
earlier, dating from the 1860s.

The doll on the right is dressed in a closely fitting,
one-piece evening dress of c.1880. It is made of silk
with a ribbed weave trimmed with satin and fastens
tightly with a lace at the back. There are extra tapes
inside the back breadth of the skirt to adjust the fit
of the front and the fall of the train. In every detail of
trimming and finish, this dress is a miniature of a
full-size gown, even to the triangular pocket at the
back of the skirt.

LEFT-HAND DOLL
MARKS Blue oval shop stamp on chest, with the partly legible
words *Recompense/Nadaud/Jouets*. (Jumeau type).
SIZE 17in (43cm).   HEAD Swivel neck; blue glass eyes; pierced
ears.   BODY All leather with gussets at elbows, hips and knees.
BODY STYLE C1 (page 125).

RIGHT-HAND DOLL
MARKS Unmarked (Jumeau type).   SIZE 17in (43cm).
HEAD Swivel neck; blue glass, almond-shaped eyes.   BODY All
leather with gussets at elbows, hips and knees.
BODY STYLE A1 (page 124).

With their "Blackamoor" servant in the background, these elegant ladies prepare to take tea. The one on the left is wearing a fine wool dress of 1878–80 trimmed with lace. The bodice has a point at the front waist and longer square tails. Over her matching skirt is a drape trimmed with a large bow at the back of the knee. The train has a square end. Her bronze kid boots, which have flat heels, fasten with laces and have a buckle at the toe. The facial features and hands of this Simonne doll closely resemble those of some early Simon & Halbig dolls.

The lady on the right wears a promenade dress of about 1885, made from satin and with contrast facing to the train. The comparative simplicity and the waistcoat-like insertion to the bodice are typical of the styles of the mid-1880s.

The servant is also illustrated on pages 28–9, where details of his dress and body style are given.

LEFT-HAND DOLL
MARKS Unmarked (Simonne type). SIZE 15in (38cm).
HEAD Swivel neck; blue glass eyes. BODY Leather over wood; bisque forearms; tenon joints at shoulders, hips and knees; loose leather over elbow joint. BODY STYLE R1 (page 132).

RIGHT-HAND DOLL
MARKS Unmarked (Jumeau type). SIZE 15in (38cm).
HEAD Swivel neck; blue glass, almond-shaped eyes; pierced ears.
BODY All wood; tenon joints at shoulders, elbows, hips and knees; socket joints at wrists; flange joints at thigh and mid-upper arm. BODY STYLE K2 (page 129).

To take her three charges for their daily constitutional, this nanny wears a dress of fine, but firmly woven, wool, with an additional matching shoulder cape. The front-button bodice is protected with a linen bib apron, and the long, tight sleeves, with their oversleeves, are held with draw tapes at the top and fastened with buttons at the wrists. Both the bodice and sleeves are embroidered with small red crosses, as are the pockets and the fancy-knitted wool petticoat. This, together with the plain petticoat, front-fastening chemise and plain-knitted wool stockings, comprise her underwear. She also wears a mid-19th-century cotton nightcap trimmed with tucks and flat black leather shoes with a silk bow at the toe. The use of the red cruciform monogram, the quality of the sewing and the type of dress suggest that the doll might have been dressed as a needlework set-piece in a convent during the 1880s.

The girl on the left is in a silk dress of the mid-1880s. The loose-cut shape, held with bands of gauging at shoulder and waist, shows the influence of the new relaxed attitude to children's clothing. Her forward tilted, peak-brimmed hat, trimmed with artificial flowers, is en suite, and she wears brown leather, side-button boots with high heels. This doll is also illustrated on pages 42–3.

On the right of the group is a girl wearing a silk-trimmed coat dress of c.1880, in line very similar to the striped silk dress worn by the doll in the centre. The coat dress has satin facings with mock button fastening, and at the back the skirt is attached at hip level where it is trimmed with a draped blue satin bow. Her small, narrow-brimmed, satin hat, is en suite and is worn tilted forward, and her high-heeled blue satin boots are stitched on. This doll is also illustrated on pages 50–1.

THE NANNY
MARKS Incised *E. Déposé B.* on shoulder-plate (probably E. Barrois). SIZE 16½in (42cm). HEAD Swivel neck; blue glass eyes; pierced ears. BODY All leather with gussets at elbows, hips and knees. BODY STYLE A1 (page 124).

LEFT-HAND DOLL
MARKS Unmarked. SIZE 12in (30cm). HEAD Fixed neck; blue glass eyes; pierced ears. BODY All leather with gussets at elbows, hips and knees. BODY STYLE A1 (page 124).

CENTRE DOLL
MARKS Unmarked (Jumeau type). SIZE 9½in (24cm). HEAD Swivel neck; pale blue glass eyes; pierced ears. BODY All leather; no gussets. BODY STYLE N2 (page 130).

RIGHT-HAND DOLL
MARKS Unmarked. SIZE 14in (36cm). HEAD Swivel neck; blue glass eyes; pierced ears. BODY Bisque arms and lower legs. Carton (cardboard) torso extending from shoulders to knees and intended to contain *dragées* (sugar almonds). Access was obtained by pulling off the lid attached to the lower legs. Dolls of this type (often called "candy containers" by collectors) were given at christening ceremonies. For many centuries it was the custom in France to distribute *dragées* at christenings, and Felix Egrefeuil, a doll maker in Paris, patented a doll in 1865 that held almonds or other sweets; he called it *Baptême*. BODY STYLE M2 (page 130).

Illustrated above and opposite is a doll
contemplating her extensive and fashionable
wardrobe of c.1863. Here she is wearing only her
lace-trimmed lawn underwear, a chenille snood and
high-heeled, lace-up boots, trimmed at the calf with
tassels. Her two walking outfits are of identical style
– one of figured poplin trimmed with applied silk,
the other of striped silk trimmed with braid. Each
outfit has a waist-length flared jacket, an ankle-
length gored skirt, with pleats to give additional
fullness at the back, and a lace-trimmed and tucked
muslin blouse. Her silk afternoon dress has a belt
with pendant trimming, and extra swing is given to
the dress by a buckram lining with additional facing
at the hem. Similar dresses are illustrated in
contemporary fashion journals. Among her
accessories are bonnets with high oval brims and at
least two sets of underwear, with a range of gored
and trained petticoats, dressing jackets and a
nightcap but no nightgown.

MARKS Incised on shoulder-plate: *E. Déposé B.* (probably
E. Barrois). SIZE 16in (41cm). DATE *c*.1860. HEAD Straight-
flange neck; dark-grey glass eyes; pierced ears. BODY Leather
torso and legs with gussets at hips; leather-over-wood knees and
upper-arms; bisque arms; tenon joints at shoulders and knees.
BODY STYLE M3 (page 130).

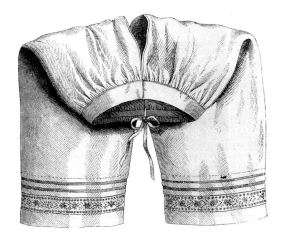

Here, kneeling by the trunk, the doll is wearing a white cotton snood and chemise with matching split drawers from one of her two sets of underwear. The other pair of drawers, one of the gored petticoats, a night cap and a blouse are pinned to the wall. On the stand is her morning dress in the smoothly fitted, unwaisted "princess-line" that was introduced in 1862–3 and had become generally fashionable by the mid-1860s.

In front of her are her high-heeled scarlet lace-up boots. They are labelled on the soles; so are her other pair, which is made from brown calf. Over the edge of the trunk may be seen her crochet cape-hood, bonnet and travelling handbag (with swivel clasps and lined with purple leather), as well as a white "fox" fur, which may have come from a later outfit. On the ground lie her reticule, made of silk knitted with beads, her silk parasol with its bone handle, whalebone ribs and brass fittings, and her fan of bone with silk leaves painted with flowers.

Preparing her charges for bed, this nursemaid wears a lawn blouse, a skirt with a woven check and a bib-apron with a matching openwork border. Her walking out dress, which is not shown and dates from c.1865, is made of silk and wool mixture in a fine black check on a grey ground. It consists of a loose-fitting jacket and a knee-length overskirt, flared at the front and pleated at the back. The borders are pointed and faced with crimson silk; tags of the same ribbon, attached to milk glass buttons shaped like flowers, trim the shoulders. The underskirt has a deep-kilted frill of fine scarlet wool, which shows at the hem, and it is supported with the padded bands on the white cotton petticoat worn beneath. The boots are of black satin and lace in the front.

The lady wears a black velvet bodice and pork-pie hat of the early 1860s.

The three dolls in foreground cannot be classified as fashion dolls; they have been included to complete the picture. The doll standing behind the bath is 11in (28cm) tall. She is all bisque, with a solid dome head, and is jointed at hips and shoulders. The doll in the bath is 7½in (19cm) tall. All bisque, she has an incised 2½ on her head and torso. The swivel joint at the waist makes her quite rare. She also has joints at shoulders and hips, and has moulded shoes and socks. The doll sitting in front of bath is an all-bisque character doll.

THE NURSEMAID

MARKS Blue Rohmer stamp on chest. SIZE 19in (48cm).
HEAD Straight-flange neck; blue glass eyes. BODY All leather with bisque forearms; gussets at hips; leather-over-wood tenon joints at shoulders; socket joints at elbows and knees. Metal eyelet holes in torso for stocking supports. BODY STYLE Q3 (page 132).

THE LADY

MARKS Incised 4 on shoulder and head (F. Gaultier type). SIZE 19in (48cm). HEAD Swivel neck; pale blue eyes; pierced ears. BODY All wood with tenon joints at shoulders, elbows, wrists, hips, knees and ankles; flange joints at waist and mid-thigh. BODY STYLE K1 (page 129).

CHILD ON BED

MARKS Incised F.G. on top-rear of head. SIZE 12in (30cm). HEAD Swivel neck; blue eyes; pierced ears. BODY Rare twill-over-wood body with bisque forearms and lower legs; tenon joints at shoulders, elbows, hips and knees. BODY STYLE B1 (page 124).

This lady, accompanied by a child, is exercising her Borzoi dog. She is wearing a summer dress of 1869–70, consisting of a knee-length taffeta overskirt, trimmed with lace and braid, which is draped at the back and worn over a striped muslin petticoat. The trimming at the waist has a square end rather like an apron. It is possible that there was once a blouse to fill in the low neckline and the short, wide, turned back sleeves. She also wears a narrow-brimmed straw hat.

The girl is wearing a braid-trimmed, striped ribbed cotton summer dress of c.1865. The overdress, which has a gored and flared skirt, is worn over a red flannel underdress pinked at the hem. It is mounted on glazed calico for extra stiffness and gets additional support from a striped buckram petticoat. Her wide-brimmed straw braid sailor hat is en suite. She wears front-lacing, beige leather boots with high heels.

THE LADY
MARKS Unmarked (possibly Huret). SIZE 17in (43cm).
DATE c.1870. HEAD Straight-flange neck; brown glass eyes; pierced ears. BODY All leather with gussets at elbows, hips and knees. BODY STYLE A1 (page 124).

THE CHILD
MARKS Unmarked (Simonne type). SIZE 13in (33cm).
DATE c.1870. HEAD Swivel neck; blue glass eyes; pierced ears.
BODY All leather with gussets at hips and knees; bisque arms with tenon joints at shoulders. BODY STYLE C2 (page 125).

Standing behind the chaise longue is a lady wearing a cotton print morning dress of c.1868. The semi-fitted jacket is hip length, and the matching skirt is cut fairly full with a plain front and a gathered back; it has a frill around the hem. The hem of the jacket, the cuffs and the skirt have an applied gathered trimming. She wears a lace cap on her head.

The daughter wears a tartan overdress of c.1865 made of fine, stiff wool. The full, box-pleated skirt and a velvet ribbon belt, trimmed with a bow, are worn over a cotton blouse. "Pinafore" skirts such as this were useful and popular girls' wear in the mid-1860s. Her straw sailor hat is trimmed with a tartan ribbon. Her shoes are made from black patent leather, fastened with an ankle band, and they are trimmed with a silk rosette at the toe. Her handbag is made from red leather, lined in red and trimmed with brass studs. It has rings and clasp of the same metal.

THE MOTHER
MARKS Incised *E. Déposé B.* on shoulder-plate.
SIZE 20in (51cm). HEAD Fixed neck; blue glass eyes; sheepskin wig. BODY Pink leather from waist down, with pink leather arms; no gussets; the upper portion of the body is carton.
BODY STYLE F2 (page 126).

THE DAUGHTER
MARKS Incised *B.S.* on shoulder-plate. SIZE 17½in (44cm). HEAD Fixed neck; cobalt blue, glass eyes. BODY All wood with tenon joints at shoulders, elbows, hips and knees; flange joints at waist and mid-thigh.
BODY STYLE O3 (page 131).

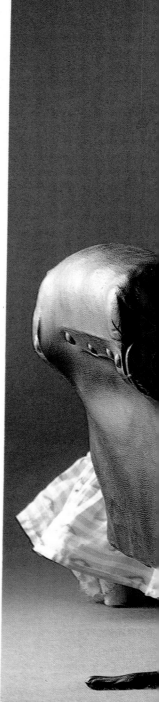

Getting ready to take tea with her companion, the lady on the left is wearing a seaside walking dress of c.1878, made from fine, stiff wool trimmed with lace. It has a tight bodice, cut without a waistseam, with ribbon bows to mask the front fastening, and is ankle length and slightly draped at the back. The matching sleeveless jacket is panelled at the back for a smooth fit; it has patch pockets, which, like the shoulders, are trimmed with ribbon bows. This outfit is a good example of the comparatively comfortable resort and sport clothes that were becoming acceptable by the late 1870s. The lady's long hair is kept tidy with a net snood, held at the crown with a silk ribbon. Her high-heeled boots have elastic sides and are made from black leather with glacé toes. Impressed on the soles are the marks CC and 2. Her complete set of underwear includes a pink-bound white corset, boned and gored, and stitched in red.

The doll on the right is wearing a dress made recently in the style of the period from re-used late 19th-century material.

The table cloth, which is fixed to the table is decorated with hand-painted roses. The blue silk, buttoned furniture is from the collection of Jackie Jacobs.

LEFT-HAND DOLL
MARKS Unmarked (F. Gaultier type). SIZE 14½in (37cm).
DATE c.1880. HEAD Swivel neck; grey glass eyes; pierced ears.
BODY All leather with gussets at elbows, hips and knees.
BODY STYLE A3 (page 124).

RIGHT-HAND DOLL
MARKS Incised *Bru* on shoulder-plate. SIZE 15in (38cm).
HEAD Swivel neck; blue glass eyes. BODY All leather with gussets at elbows, hips and knees. BODY STYLE A3 (page 124).

With two bridesmaids to accompany her, the bride is wearing a dress of c.1875. It is made of silk taffeta trimmed with embroidered net and orange blossom. She has a diagonal-fastening, long-waisted jacket bodice trimmed with wound silk buttons, pleated at the back of the waist and trimmed with a made-up bow; her skirt has an apron drape under which are wide ties holding the puff that heads the long sweeping train. On the border is an applied gathered trimming and two rows of frills. The veil is of embroidered net. Her shoes are white kid, low cut and with pink rosettes at the toes. The soles are impressed with the marks CC and 4.

An interesting feature of this costume is the bustle, which consists of skirt-length pleats of stiffened net with a small glazed cotton cushion to provide extra fullness at the hips.

The bridesmaid in the centre is in a summer day dress of c.1868. The tucked blouse has medium-wide sleeves trimmed with frills at the elbow; the skirt is very full at the back where it is tightly gathered at the waist, the line being emphasized by the bands of frilled trimming, vertical at the front and exaggerating the breadth at the back. Around the shoulders is a matching mantle, which crosses to tie at the back. An interesting accessory are her garters, which are made from blue elastic fastened with gilt clasps. Her high-heeled slippers are of white satin, and they are trimmed at the toes with rosettes.

The bridesmaid on the right is in an organdy dress of 1850–5, which is earlier than the doll. The dress has a long, back-laced, pointed bodice and a double skirt mounted over glazed cotton. The bodice is gauged at the front, and at the shoulders deep wings almost conceal the sleeves, which are trimmed with a deep frill to the elbow. Matching ribbon rosettes trim the dress at the shoulders, elbows and wrists. Her hat probably dates from c.1900.

THE BRIDE
MARKS Unmarked (Jumeau type). SIZE 17½in (44cm).
DATE c.1870. HEAD Swivel neck; blue glass eyes; pierced ears.
BODY All leather with gussets at elbows, hips and knees.
BODY STYLE A1 (page 124).

CENTRE BRIDESMAID
MARKS Incised *B.S.* on shoulder-plate. SIZE 17½in (44cm).
DATE c.1860. HEAD Fixed neck; cobalt blue glass eyes.
BODY Leather over wood with tenon joints at shoulders, elbows, hips and knees; bisque forearms. BODY STYLE O1 (page 131).

RIGHT-HAND BRIDESMAID
MARKS Red shop label reading *Remond Seur. rue Neuve de Champs* on torso (Jumeau type). SIZE 16in (41cm). HEAD Swivel neck; blue glass eyes; pierced ears. BODY All leather with gussets at elbows and hips. BODY STYLE N3 (page 130).

With her bridesmaids in the background, the bride is wearing a dress of the mid-1880s of silk with a ribbed weave, trimmed with lace and orange blossom. The tightly fitting bodice, boned and padded, fastens at the back. The front of the skirt is pleated, and there is an overdress, its puffed shape controlled with internal tapes, which extends into a square-ended train. The underdress is attached to a silk petticoat, stiffened with a bustle of starched cotton, which is stitched to it. The embroidered net veil is decorated with wax orange blossom. The high-heeled, white satin shoes are low cut and have a bow at the instep.

The groom wears a full dress cut-away suit of the late 19th century. His pleated shirt has satin-covered buttons, and he has a white tie and a silk plush top hat.

THE BRIDE
MARKS Green Simonne stamp on chest.   SIZE 17½in (44cm).
DATE *c.*1860.   HEAD Swivel neck; cobalt blue glass eyes.
BODY Leather over wood with tenon joints at shoulders, elbows, hips and knees; bisque forearms.   BODY STYLE O1 (page 131).

THE GROOM
MARKS Unmarked.   SIZE 17in (43cm).   HEAD Swivel neck; cobalt blue glass eyes; pierced ears.   BODY Pink kid; no gussets; mitten-type hands.   BODY STYLE F1 (page 126).

Unable to cope single-handedly with her corset, this lady sought help. The corset is of blue cotton twill, lined with white; it is closely boned and fastens at the back with a lace threaded through metal mounted eyelets. Beneath it can be seen her underwear, which is lace-trimmed lawn of the finest quality. The fit of her evening chemise can be adjusted with buttons at the shoulders. In wear it would be tucked into the matching close-fitting knee-length drawers with the split gusset, which were conventional wear for the adult woman of the 1880s.

The husband wears a full dress suit, a late 19th-century cut-away of fine cloth with unusual low-cut, satin-faced lapels and rounded coat tails. His collarless waistcoat is made from white satin and fastens with "pearl" buttons; he has a stiff-bosomed shirt with pearl studs, a wing collar and a white tie.

The 19th-century bed is 33in (84cm) high, and the carved and turned wood is decorated in gold leaf. The pure silk brocade drapes are completely original.

THE LADY

MARKS Incised *R. C. Déposé* on shoulder-plate (rare type of doll). A doll of this type was patented by Rodiquet & Cordonnier in 1880. SIZE 16½in (42cm). HEAD Swivel neck; blue glass eyes; pierced ears. BODY Leather with bisque arms and lower legs; one arm straight and one bent; moulded bosom; holes in soles of feet for original stand. (This type of doll is occasionally found with two straight arms or two bent arms; also with moulded shoes.) BODY STYLE C3 (page 125).

THE HUSBAND

MARKS Unmarked. SIZE 18in (46cm). HEAD Swivel neck; cobalt blue glass eyes; pierced ears. BODY Leather over wood with bisque forearms and lower legs; tenon joints at shoulders, elbows, hips and knees. BODY STYLE G3 (page 127).

Reclining on a couch, this elegant lady wears a lace-trimmed fine wool summer dress of c.1868. It has a short fitted bodice with wide, elbow-length, flared sleeves extending into longer square-edged tails. The matching skirt is tightly pleated at the back, where it is trimmed with frills from hips to hem. Her cap dates from the 1880s, as may her feather fan with its wooden sticks. To complete the ensemble, she wears part of a set of "pearl and sapphire" jewellery, consisting of a brooch, ear-rings, watch, hairpin and pendant necklace.

MARKS Unmarked (Bru type).   SIZE 23in (58cm).   HEAD Swivel neck; blue glass eyes with moulded lower lids; pierced ears.
BODY All leather; no gussets; separated toes.
BODY STYLE E1 (page 126) but no gussets.

The doll holding the apple is wearing a simple summer dress of check muslin dating from about 1865.

The other doll wears a summer day dress of printed cotton of 1868–70, trimmed with white work embroidery. The knee-length jacket has a draped back, the skirt is gathered at the back. The gathered cotton hat is later, dating from about 1900. Pinned to her dress is a fob watch with an "enamel" back.

DOLL WITH APPLE
MARKS Unmarked; attributed Jumeau.   SIZE 20in (51cm).
HEAD Swivel neck; blue glass eyes; pierced ears.   BODY All wood with tenon joints at shoulders, elbows, hips and knees; flange joints at mid-upper arm and mid-thigh; bisque hands.
BODY STYLE K2 but with bisque hands (page 129). (*Jackie Jacobs*)

RIGHT-HAND DOLL
MARKS Unmarked; attributed Jumeau.   SIZE 21½in (55cm).
HEAD Swivel neck; blue glass eyes; pierced ears (sometimes found with applied ears).   BODY All leather with gussets at elbows, hips and knees; separate stitched toes.   BODY STYLE E1 (page 126).

To take an elderly relative out for some fresh air this lady wears a promenade dress of c.1880. Made of velvet trimmed with lace, it consists of a tightly fitting jacket with gathered tails and fastened from neck to hip with closely spaced globular glass buttons. The matching skirt has a box pleated front and a short train trimmed with a pleated band and a puffed and gathered drape. Matching satin bows trim the back of the jacket and train. Her draped muslin hat is trimmed with a matching ostrich feather; the white "fox" fur and "ermine" muff may be of a slightly later date. The underwear is from the 1880s and includes a petticoat that has a bustle mounted above two tiers of lace-trimmed, pleated muslin frills. Her boots are of bronze kid, high heeled and with side fastening. The figure 5 is impressed into the soles.

Sitting in the Bath chair, which comes from the collection of Jackie Jacobs, is a German character doll.

MARKS Incised *L. Déposé 4 D.* on shoulder-plate.
SIZE 18½in (47cm). DATE *c.*1870. HEAD Swivel neck; blue glass, almond-shaped eyes; pierced ears. BODY All leather with gussets at hips and knees; bisque arms with tenon joints at shoulders.
BODY STYLE C2 (page 125).

Dressed for a day at the races, the doll on the left wears a striped silk dress of c.1876 with a long-waisted jacket bodice fastened with metal buttons. Her fashionably cut skirt, with apron drape at the front, is caught asymmetrically with a large blue bow on the intricately draped back, where a loose drape, which merges with the short train, is framed with two gathered bands of blue ribbon. Her high-heeled boots are fastened with double buttons and loops at the front. To complete her ensemble she carries a gilt metal lorgnette suspended from a brooch and a black cotton umbrella with metal ribs. Her silk velvet hat may well be of a later date.

The other doll wears a fashionably close-fitting dress of c.1878 and carries a frilled parasol of the period and wears a straw bonnet.

LEFT-HAND DOLL
MARKS Unmarked (Jumeau type). SIZE 18in (46cm).
HEAD Swivel neck; blue glass eyes; pierced ears. BODY Leather over wood with bisque forearms and lower legs; tenon joints at shoulders, elbows, hips and knees. BODY STYLE G3 (page 127). (*Jackie Jacobs*)

RIGHT-HAND DOLL
MARKS Incised *F.G.* on shoulder-plate and *4* on back of head and shoulder. SIZE 18½in (47cm). HEAD Swivel neck; blue glass eyes; pierced ears. BODY All wood; tenon joints at shoulders, elbows, hips and knees; socket joints at wrists; flange joints at mid-upper arm and mid-thigh. BODY STYLE P3 (page 131).

Standing before a sedan chair and waiting to be taken to a ball, this lady is dressed in a court or formal ball dress of c.1865. The bodice, with its flared epaulets, and the train are made from ribbed silk trimmed with applied silk braid. The front is covered with gathered bands of tulle arranged in diamond shapes and trimmed with pearls and blue satin bows. The dress, which laces at the back, is lined with white silk and trimmed around the edges with a pleated frill.

An interesting accessory are the doll's stockings, which are of silk, reaching to the thigh with a lace pattern from calf to instep. Her garters are of blue silk ribbon. She wears white satin high-heeled court shoes, which have blue and white ribbon ruches at the toe.

MARKS Röhmer; oval green stamp on torso. SIZE 18in (46cm). HEAD Straight-flange neck; blue glass eyes. BODY All leather with gussets at hips; tenon joint at shoulders; leather-over-wood socket joints at knees; two eyelet-holes in torso, threaded with tapes, which support the stockings. BODY STYLE L2 (page 129). (*Elsie Potter*)

The child, who is perched on a chair to reach its mother, is in a striped silk coat dress of the mid-1880s, with a frill at the back and pockets at the hips. It must have been intended for winter wear because it is padded and there is an adjustable collar of gathered silk.

The mother on the other hand is wearing a summer dress, of c.1868, of white muslin with a plain bodice and flared cuffs. The skirt is plain at the front but gathered at the back, where it flows into a short train. This fashionable line is supported by a half-length bustle petticoat of stiff pleated muslin. She also wears a silk mantle of the same date and carries a bone and silk fan painted with flowers.

THE CHILD
MARKS Incised *F.G.* top-back of crown.   SIZE 12in (30cm).
HEAD Swivel neck; blue glass eyes; pierced ears.   BODY Twill over wood; bisque forearms and lower legs; tenon joints at shoulders, elbows, hips and knees.   BODY STYLE B1 (page 124).

THE MOTHER
MARKS Square green shop stamp reading *A la Poupée de Nuremberg, Lavallée Peronne, 21 rue Choiseul, Paris.*
SIZE 17in (43cm).   HEAD Swivel neck; pale blue glass eyes; pierced ears.   BODY All leather; bisque forearms; leather-over-wood tenon joints at shoulders and elbows.   BODY STYLE J2 but arms K3 (page 129). (Elsie Potter)

The gutta-percha body of this doll bears a Huret stamp. The bisque head, with painted eyes, has a swivel neck, and the body has tenon joints at elbows, hips and knees. The small doll, which is also illustrated on page 111, is 11in (28cm) tall, and is a Huret-type doll. (Jackie Jacobs)

This handsome couple are not wearing exactly contemporaneous clothes. The lady is in a fashionable dress of 1863–5, with the triangular "Swiss" waistband with a bow at the back, and low neck and puffed sleeves, trimmed with lace. The skirt is set in broad, double box pleats, wide enough to need the support of the crinoline petticoat of figured cotton, stiffened with cane or wire hoops. Her underwear also includes a pair of wide, multi-tucked split drawers, their fullness so characteristic of the 1860s. The boots, made of leather to match the colour of the dress, fasten with a front lacing. The jewellery and hair decoration, but not the fan, are of a later period.

The gentleman is dressed in the style of the 1870s. He wears a full-length woollen dressing gown with attached cape and silk-lined hood. It fastens with silk-covered buttons. His night shirt of white cotton reaches to his ankles, and the high collar, the long straight sleeves and the full length button stand are edged with white embroidery.

In his outfit also are knee-length cotton split drawers, ribbed brown stockings and front-fastening lace-up brown leather shoes. His shirt is a style that rarely survives in a full-size version; it is of cotton printed in alternating stripes of tiny polka dots and floral trails. It has a pleated front collar and fastens with small pearl buttons.

THE LADY
MARKS Incised *H* on the top-back of head. SIZE 19in (48cm).
HEAD Swivel neck; blue glass eyes; pierced ears. BODY All leather with gussets at hips and knees; wood arms with tenon joints at shoulders, elbows and wrists. BODY STYLE O2 (page 131).
(*Jackie Jacobs*)

THE GENTLEMAN
MARKS Incised *J. Déposé* top-front of crown; attributed Bru.
SIZE 23in (58cm). HEAD Swivel neck; brown glass eyes. BODY All leather with gussets at elbows, hips and knees; separate stitched toes. BODY STYLE E1 (page 126).

Surrounded by her pet dogs, this doll is wearing a
walking dress of c.1880, its closely fitting lines
emphasized with trimmings of striped silk. The
bodice fits tightly to the body, and the overskirt is
gathered in the front and smoothly panelled at the
back. The smooth line, so characteristic of the 1880s,
is enhanced with bows. The closely fitting bonnet
trimmed with artificial flowers is of the same date.

MARKS Incised *F.G.* on shoulder-plate and 4 on back of head and
shoulder.   SIZE 18½in (47cm).   HEAD Swivel neck; blue glass eyes;
pierced ears.   BODY All wood; tenon joints at shoulders, elbows,
hips and knees; socket joints at wrists; flange joints mid-upper
arm and mid-thigh.   BODY STYLE P3 (page 131).

A LA GALERIE VIVIENNE
4, rue N.^{vo} des Petits Champs.

MAISON GUILLARD

RÉMOND Successeur.

FOURNISSEUR
DE S.A.I. LE PRINCE IMPÉRIAL
JOUETS
JEUX DE SOCIÉTÉ
PARIS

The child shown in the photograph (opposite above) could well have been the original owner of this doll, for the dress the child is wearing is a copy of the doll's. The trade card (above left) was almost certainly presented at the time the doll was bought – although the doll portrayed is different, the gown is identical – and is fairly conclusive proof that the dress is original to the doll.

The gown that the doll is wearing is a very fashionable promenade dress of c.1865. It is made of satin and silk with a ribbed weave, and the borders are trimmed with gilt braid mounted over red silk and trimmed with gilt braided beads. The hem measures 80in (2 metres). The bodice has a high neck and long sleeves, and over it is worn the loose jacket with its very wide, flared sleeves. The en suite bonnet, with its high, oval brim, is made from machine-made lace and trimmed with artificial flowers and beads. She carries a parasol and a bone and silk fan painted with flowers.

This doll is also illustrated on pages 30–1.

MARKS Unmarked, but very rare mould. SIZE 19in (48cm).
DATE *c*.1865. HEAD Swivel neck; cobalt blue glass eyes; pierced ears. BODY Leather over wood with tenon joints at shoulders, elbows, hips and knees; bisque forearms; moulded bosom as in C3. This type of body sometimes also has arms as in C3.
BODY STYLE O1 (page 131).

91

Posed rather austerely in front of a vase of white flowers, both these dolls are wearing crinolines of c.1868. The lady on the left is in a dress of c.1868 of striped silk, trimmed with lace, consisting of a hip-length jacket bodice and an overskirt of bias-cut panels, draped and pleated at the back. The underskirt, which is of similar cut, has a stiff lining. She has a hat en suite – a wired tulle coronet

trimmed with beads and berries. The high-heeled boots are of bronze kid and have elastic gussets.

The lady on the right wears a promenade dress of 1867–8. It has a bodice and draped overskirt of figured silk faced with satin, split and draped at each side where it is joined by the two buttoned bands. The underskirt is made from ribbon-striped watered silk and gathered at the centre back. Her low-heeled

boots are of bronze kid, fastened with buttons and trimmed with tassels at the top; impressed in the sole are the marks 4 and BEAUDELOT A PARIS. The hat may be of a later date.

LEFT-HAND DOLL
MARKS Simonne stamp on chest bearing the address *rue de Rivoli 188*. SIZE 18in (46cm). HEAD Straight-flange neck; cobalt blue glass eyes; pierced ears. BODY All leather with gussets at hips and knees; bisque arms. BODY STYLE J2 (page 128). (*Elsie Potter*)

RIGHT-HAND DOLL
MARKS Huret stamp on chest bearing the address *Boulevard Montmartre 22*. SIZE 15½in (39cm). HEAD Fixed neck; painted blue eyes; pierced ears. BODY Gutta-percha; tenon joints at shoulders, hips and knees. BODY STYLE H2 (page 127). (*Elsie Potter*)

Standing in front of a varied selection of dolls' hats dating from the late 19th and early 20th centuries are two girls. The one on the left wears a young girl's printed cotton dress of c.1865, with short puffed sleeves and a mid-calf length gathered skirt, its fullness enhanced by a double row of frills. Her straw hat dates from the 1880s.

The other doll wears a summer day outfit of c.1865 made from a silk gauze with a woven stripe and faced with bands of tucked silk. The jacket, which is unwaisted, flares from shoulders to hips and has wide straight sleeves. The matching skirt is gored, and its fullness is controlled by gathers at the back. The blouse, of the same date, is of lace with net insertion. It fastens down the front with cotton-covered buttons and has pearl buttons at the cuffs of the long sleeves. Her small, curly brimmed hat is of the same period. Her shoes of red morocco have square toes and are trimmed with matching ribbon.

The chair shown here is stamped Huret; *Leopold Huret is recorded as trading in dolls' furniture from 1850. The other hats date from the late 19th to the early 20th century.*

LEFT-HAND DOLL
MARKS Incised *Huret, 56 rue de la Boet* on back of torso.
SIZE 17in (43cm).   HEAD Swivel neck; blue glass eyes; this doll does not have a bisque shoulder-plate; the head is mounted directly on to the body.   BODY All metal with socket joints at shoulders, elbows, wrists, waist, hips and knees.
BODY STYLE H3 (page 127). (*Elsie Potter*)

RIGHT-HAND DOLL
MARKS Unmarked; attributed Huret.   SIZE 17in (43cm).
HEAD Swivel neck; blue glass eyes.   BODY All wood with tenon joints at shoulders, elbows, wrists, hips, knees and ankles; flange joints at waist and mid-thigh.   BODY STYLE L1 (page 129). (*Elsie Potter*)

Dressed in her lace-trimmed muslin dress of c.1868, this doll is posed in the conservatory. Her gown has a jacket bodice and an overskirt with a draped back over a low-necked underdress with a double skirt. She carries an imitation ivory fan painted with roses and forget-me-nots, as well as a parasol of about the same date with a cotton satin cover, a brass knob with an impressed star design and metal ribs.

MARKS Incised *E.B.* on shoulder-plate. SIZE 15½in (39cm).
HEAD Fixed neck; painted blue eyes; pierced ears. BODY All leather; no gussets. BODY STYLE F1 (page 126).

Protecting herself with a parasol, the doll on the left is wearing a summer walking dress of c.1875. It is made of starched cotton trimmed with white work embroidery and bands of lace-edged pleating. The jacket bodice is hip length and there is an overskirt draped at the back. Her forward-tilted, corded silk Tyrolean hat is trimmed with artificial flowers. Her parasol, which is about the same date as her outfit, has a silk cover, a turned handle, in a substance closely resembling ivory, and whalebone ribs.

The doll on the right is also illustrated on pages 102–3, where details of her gown and body style are given.

MARKS Incised *4* on neck and shoulder.   SIZE 17in (43cm).
HEAD Swivel neck; blue glass eyes; pierced ears.   BODY Pressed leather; tenon joints at shoulders, elbows, hips and knees; a rare type of body, patented by V. Clément in 1866.
BODY STYLE G2 (page 127).

Not only wearing contrasting colours, these two dolls also represent a difference of thirty years in their style of outfits. The child is dressed as a girl of the mid-1880s. Her knee-length, satin, princess-line coat is caught with ribbons across the chest and worn over a matching pleated underdress. Her stockings are of matching silk, and she has flat-heeled bronze kid shoes, which fasten with ankle bands and have cut steel rosettes at the toe. Her outfit also includes two hats – a matching plush bonnet with a high, curved brim and a summer straw hat with a medium-wide brim faced with plum-coloured satin and a silk ribbon band.

The lady wears a velvet jacket of the later 1850s. It is close-fitting but flared at the hips and with wide sleeves. Trimmed with applied silk and "jet" motifs, it has a matching bead fringe. It fastens with hooks and eyes. With it she wears a 1890s-style satin bonnet, trimmed with ostrich feather. On the leather back of this doll is written a partial history of its ownership: "Marie given to K.C.B. 1869. Lent to P.C.B. then D.M.M. in 1899. & K.J.M. in 1906. P.K.M. 1925. B.W.M. 1940."

THE CHILD

MARKS Blue oval Rohmer shop stamp on body.
SIZE 17½in (44cm). HEAD Straight-flange neck joint; painted blue eyes. BODY All leather with bisque arms; tenon joints at shoulders; leather-over-wood socket joints at knees; gussets at hips; eyelet holes in torso for tapes to support stockings.
BODY STYLE L2 (page 129).

THE LADY

MARKS Blue oval Rohmer shop stamp on body.
SIZE 18½in (47cm). HEAD Swivel neck; blue glass eyes; pierced ears. BODY All leather with bisque forearms; gussets at hips; tenon joints at shoulders; leather-over-wood socket joints at elbows and knees. BODY STYLE Q3 (page 132).

Both these ladies preparing to take tea together are wearing promenade dresses. The doll on the left is in a promenade dress of the late 1870s. This has a front-fastening, corset-like, fitted bodice with long, square-ended tails and a band at the low hip line, and a draped and puffed square-ended train. The lace on her skirt matches that on the petticoat and on the low-heeled satin shoes. Her satin hat is on a wired foundation and is trimmed with pink and purple flowers.

The doll on the right wears a one-piece, fitted promenade dress of fine wool, decorated with a gathered frill at the low hip line. Bands of tucks, gathers and pleats trim the long-trained skirt. There are rows of satin-covered buttons running from neck to waist on both the front and back of the bodice; button trimming, which added interest to the back of the bodice, was a fashion feature of the 1870s. Her hat, which dates from the early 1870s, is trimmed with feathers. This doll, wearing the same gown, is also illustrated on page 99.

LEFT-HAND DOLL
MARKS Incised *F.G.* on shoulder-plate.   SIZE 18in (46cm).
HEAD Swivel neck; pale blue glass eyes; pierced ears.   BODY All leather; no gussets.   BODY STYLE N2 (page 130).

RIGHT-HAND DOLL
MARKS Signed *Rochard* inside shoulder-plate; patented 1868.
SIZE 17½in (44cm).   HEAD Swivel neck; blue glass eyes; pierced ears.   BODY All leather with bisque forearms; gussets at elbows, hips and knees; glass "pendant" inset into the front of shoulder-plate.   BODY STYLE I2 (page 128). (*Elsie Potter*)

Sheltering together from the rain, this couple are both wearing outfits of the 1880s. The woman's promenade outfit is made from figured velvet and trimmed with fur. The jacket, fitted and hip length, is worn over a skirt, open to show the pleated satin underskirt. Her hat is of matching velvet. However, her handbag of morocco, fastening and studded with gilt, and her umbrella, with its turned bone handle, date from the 1870s.

The man's formal suit of the 1880s is in the finest and smoothest of cloth. It is double-breasted, four-button fastening and has square ended tails. His trousers have a centre fly fastening. The starched shirt front is of fine lawn and fastens with china buttons. His waistcoat is of ribbed cotton and has a shawl collar, while the black satin tie is arranged in a ready-made bow. His hat is of silk plush. The umbrella, probably also of the 1880s, has a cotton twill cover, a stained wooden crook handle and metal ribs. His boots, however, are those of a lady of the period: brown leather with high heels and a side fastening.

THE WOMAN
MARKS Incised *E* on head and shoulders; attributed "smiling" Bru.   SIZE 15in (38cm).   HEAD Swivel neck; grey glass eyes; pierced ears.   BODY All wood; tenon joints at shoulders, elbows, wrists, knees and ankles; socket joint at waist.
BODY STYLE E2 (page 126). (*Richard Wright*)

THE MAN
MARKS Incised *F* on back of head and shoulders; attributed "smiling" Bru.   SIZE 18in (46cm).   HEAD Swivel neck; blue glass eyes; pierced ears.   BODY All leather with gussets at hips and knees; wood arms with tenon joints at shoulders, elbows and wrists.   BODY STYLE O2 (page 131).

Both dressed in brown, these two dolls watch the small doll read by candlelight. The doll on the left is wearing a plain walking dress of the late 1860s. Made from a ribbed silk and wool mixture, the outfit is faced and trimmed with velvet. The buttons are of glass "jet." The dress consists of a jacket bodice with draped overskirt, and an underskirt of re-used watered silk, plain at the front and pleated at the back. Her straw sailor hat is trimmed with flowers and faced with gathered silk. The high-heeled bronze kid shoes are unusual in that they have an elastic ankle band with a central brass clasp and adjustable loops.

The doll on the right is wearing a silk, lace-trimmed jacket and skirt of the mid-1860s. The jacket is shaped to the figure and the skirt is arranged in box pleats. She wears a pork-pie hat with ribbon streamers. The front-fastening boots are of brown leather; they have flat heels and fasten with laces.

This doll is included to illustrate the forerunners of the bisque-head fashion dolls.

LEFT-HAND DOLL
MARKS Incised *E.B.* on shoulder-plate. SIZE 14½in (37cm).
HEAD Swivel neck; cobalt blue glass eyes; pierced ears. BODY All leather with gussets at elbows, hips and knees.
BODY STYLE A1 (page 124). (*Elsie Potter*)

RIGHT-HAND DOLL
MARKS Unmarked; Rohmer type. SIZE 18in (46cm).
HEAD Glazed china; fixed neck; cobalt blue glass eyes. BODY All leather with gussets at elbows, hips and knees.
BODY STYLE A1 (page 124).

Gazing admiringly at her own reflection, this doll is in a dress of machine-made lace over silk in the style of the 1880s. An interesting feature of this outfit are the side-button boots, which are made from pink kid and have a silver buckle at the toe. Impressed on the soles of the boots are the marks 50 and AP MODES de PARIS. The set of jewels, "coral set in gilt," date from the late 1860s, and include ear-rings, a pair of bracelets, two chains for the hair, a decorative comb and a watch on a long gilt chain, the face marked Paris. She also has a pendant with an Egyptian-style central boss.

MARKS Incised *L. Déposé D.* on shoulder-plate.
SIZE 18½in (47cm).   HEAD Swivel neck; painted blue eyes.
BODY All leather with gussets at elbows, hips and knees.
BODY STYLE A1 (page 124).

The bulbous neck of this doll is typical of Huret dolls. The lower arms are bisque, and there are tenon joints at shoulders and elbows and gussets at the hips; at the knees are kid-over-wood ball and socket joints. This doll's body is, in fact, very similar to the Rohmer body illustrated on page 129. (Jackie Jacobs)

109

This unmarked but Bru-type doll is 16in (41cm) tall. The bisque head has a swivel neck; the body is leather, with gussets at hips and knees, but the arms are of wood and have tenon joints at shoulders, elbows and wrists. (Jackie Jacobs)

The dolls on the left and right of this illustration are rare child fashion dolls, both of the type manufactured by Huret. The doll on the left is 8½in (21cm) tall; the bisque head has a fixed neck and the eyes are painted; the body is leather. The doll on the right, which is 11in (28cm) tall, also has a bisque head, fixed neck and painted eyes, but the body is leather over wood with tenon joints at shoulder, elbows, hips and knees. The doll in the centre, which is not a fashion doll, is an all-bisque baby doll, manufactured by the German firm Kestner (Jackie Jacobs)

The range and variety of accessories made for fashion dolls in the latter half of the 19th century are illustrated on these and the two following page. Reproduced actual size, the objects range from binoculars to a needle case. The set of "coral and gilt" jewellery is still on its original card.

113

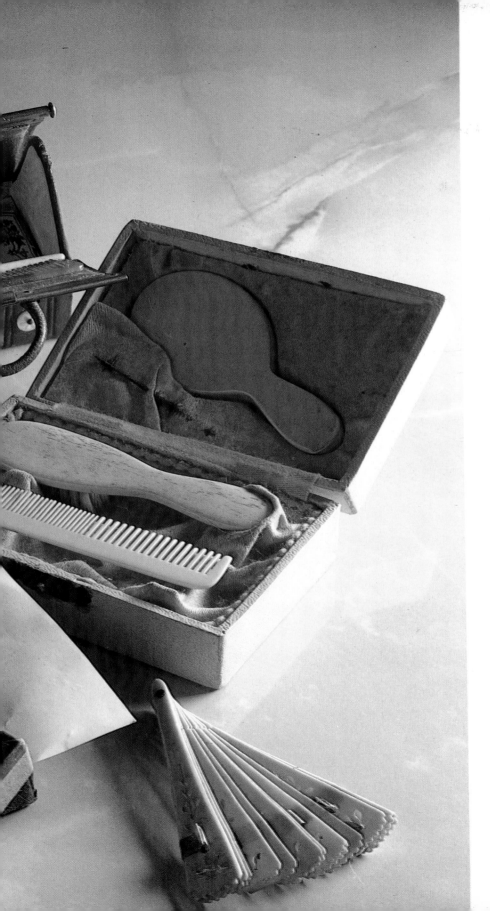

Also reproduced actual size, this group of accessories includes a set of ivory-backed hair brushes, with button hook and shoe horn, and an ivory fan. The posy of flowers is made of wax.

115

FRENCH FASHION DOLL
MANUFACTURERS AND THEIR MARKS

When an antique doll is being examined one question always arises: what marks does the doll bear that could provide a positive indication of its manufacturer? When used, doll makers' marks usually took the form of a label, surface printing or a mark incised into the bisque of the doll's head or shoulder-plate. The last is generally regarded as being the most reliable, as labels often peel off and printed marks, with the passage of time, frequently become almost indecipherable. Moreover, stamps and labels were sometimes applied by the retailer as distinct from the manufacturer. The identity of the majority of French fashion doll manufacturers, as distinct from those suppliers who purchased parts from other sources, which they then assembled and sold, is now known, and any doll with an incised or clear, printed mark of one of the known manufacturers can generally be accepted as the product of the indicated maker.

In the case of the best known manufacturers of French fashion dolls – Huret, Rohmer, Jumeau, Bru and Fernand Gaultier – marked dolls are, however, in the minority. The practise of incising porcelain with a doll maker's mark became commonplace only during the last two decades of the 19th century, but most of the dolls produced by these makers were made between 1850 and 1875, and hence few bear incised marks.

Exceptions are found among the many fashion doll heads and shoulder-plates that are incised with the initials *F.G.* These initials have, however, caused some confusion, for both the Gaultier and Gesland families at sometime or another used the initial "F," and both families were in business over the same period of time, namely between 1860 and 1915–16 (see pages 119–20).

What, however, of the doll that bears no conclusive identification in the form of a mark? Experienced collectors will instantly recognize the characteristics of a Bru or Jumeau, but for novices matters are not so simple. How can they recognize the style of a particular French fashion doll maker?

The answer to this question is precisely the same that we give to collectors seeking knowledge about 19th-century costume: "only a constant and continuing examination of all the available examples ... will finally lead to that indefinable ability to judge and assess the authenticity and quality of what one sees."

The same advice applies, of course, in any field of the fine arts or antiques. Many items bear no positive indication of the artist or craftsman, but almost every one, to the enthusiast or expert, is instantly recognizable. Enthusiastic experience is the answer, and it is sometimes amazing how quickly complete novices acquire confidence and knowledge.

A surprising number of books have been published on the subject of the antique doll, and these will aid novices on their way. (A number of titles are included in the Bibliography on page 142.) Reference can also be made to historical printed sources. Contemporary information about the manufacturers of French dolls during the 19th century is profuse yet often confusing. A large number of names appeared in such annual publications as the French Chamber of Commerce directories for Paris (the fashion doll industry was centred there), and the entries make interesting reading.

Unfortunately, the records for some years have vanished, and in some of the directories names have been inexplicably omitted. The entries themselves give rise to further complications, for the information recorded was obviously supplied by the firms concerned, and the entries sometimes read more like sales catalogues than official documents providing impartial information about the precise nature of a company's business. It is, for instance, difficult to establish beyond all doubt if the firms listed actually manufactured all, or only part, of what they sold. Gesland, for example, is known to have imported dolls' heads from Germany, and some of the major French manufacturers undoubtedly supplied heads to smaller establishments. (This form of trade is discussed more fully on pages 14–16.)

Despite such areas of confusion, those people recorded in the list that follows can reasonably be regarded as manufacturers, as they all produced the major portion of the dolls they supplied. Even when the origin of a particular head is in doubt, it is still possible that the head was modelled and produced to specifications provided by the purchasers and unique to their use.

The makers that are described in the "directory" that follows include some of the most prominent doll manufacturers who were associated with the French fashion doll trade that thrived in Paris in the 19th century and whose products are illustrated in this book.

Barrois, Madame

The Paris Chamber of Commerce directory of 1846 shows the registration of Mme. Barrois at 163 rue St Martin, Paris, but the entry was deleted in 1852. There is then a gap of a further six years before there is another entry for the same name and the same street, but at different premises.

Barrois, E.

E. Barrois is mentioned in the directories as a maker and distributor of porcelain and paste dolls' heads between 1858 and 1877, and the address at this period was 192 rue St Martin, Paris. It is interesting that the directory notes that the company also traded in German heads.

When recording the two separate entries of Barrois, it is usually the custom to state the facts and leave it at that, but the coincidence of the same name being found in the same street, together with the recorded dates, makes it difficult to believe that two entirely different firms or people were involved. E. Barrois could have been the husband or son of Mme. Barrois, or indeed the two Barrois might have been the same person who, after the six-year gap, re-registered under a different trading name.

Fashion dolls with *E. Déposé B.* incised on the shoulder-plate are generally attributed to E. Barrois. The mark may be found on dolls with fixed necks, straight-flange necks or swivel necks; the bodies may be all leather, with and without gussets, or have leather torsos and bisque arms, or leather-over-wood knees and upper arms. Dolls with the incised mark *E.B.* or *E. Déposé B.* are illustrated on pages 26–7, 56–7, 58, 64–5, 97 and 106–7. The doll illustrated on pages 64–5 is also shown on page 126 (F2).

BRU JᴺᴱR

BRU. JᴺᴱR

Bru

The history of the great French doll making firm of Bru is more fully documented than that of any other French doll manufacturer apart from Jumeau. Official records are supplemented by the company's extensive advertising. The company was active between 1866 and 1899, and during that period was under the management of three men: Casimir Bru (1866–83), H. Chevrot (1883–9) and Paul Girard (1889–99). Although Girard continued to be associated with the company after 1899, it was no longer independent but part of the Société Française de Fabrication de Bébés et Jouets (S.F.B.J.).

As early as 1866 Bru employed over thirty workers at its premises at rue St Denis, Paris; very soon, business operations also began in the rue Mauconseil. Suitable dresses for dolls were also produced in addition to the dolls themselves, and exports to America were part of the firm's business.

To record even a few of Bru's innovations in the field of doll making is beyond the scope of this book, but the company was credited with at least thirty patents, including the "Surprise" two-faced doll illustrated on page 128 (I1).

By 1885, when the new factory at Montreuil-sous-Bois was in full operation, there was hardly a material or an idea with which Bru, under the management of H. Chevrot, had not experimented in an attempt to produce new and exciting items. Not all were successful and many sank without trace. But the Bru dolls that exist today are visible proof that the company was pre-eminent in the field of doll making. Between 1885 and 1893 Bru was awarded nine gold and two silver medals in international exhibitions – further evidence of the company's success.

The bodies of fashion dolls known to have been produced by Bru vary from all leather, with gussets at elbows, hips and knees, to all leather with no gussets at all. Heads were either fixed or a swivel neck was used. Bru-type dolls – that is, those in the style of Bru but without positive identifying marks – are illustrated on pages 25, 32–3, 40–1, 42–3, 44–5, 75 and 105, and on page 126 (E1) and page 131 (O1).

Bru dolls sometimes had *B Jne et Cie.* incised on the shoulder-plate and *Déposé* incised on the shoulder; occasionally they have *Déposé* incised under the hair at the front top of the head and a letter, to denote size, on the back of the head. Fashion dolls with Bru markings are extremely rare, but two such are illustrated on pages 66–7 and 87, and on page 124 (A3) and page 131 (P2).

B.S.

A number of fine quality, French fashion dolls have the initials *B.S.* incised on the shoulder-plate. Although they all seem to have been produced by the same doll maker, there is as yet no positive evidence of the manufacturer's identity. There are, however, two main contenders to the title.

Blampoix Aîné (Senior)

Blampoix Senior produced fashion dolls in Paris between 1840 and 1870. In 1855 he obtained a patent to insert both glass and enamel eyes into porcelain dolls' heads. In 1863 a large factory was opened in Paris for the manufacture of porcelain heads, and complete, fully dressed dolls were produced.

The claim that it was the Blampoix firm that incised its dolls *B.S.* is based on the theory that Blampoix himself was known as "Blampoix Senior," but this is open to question. "Senior" is not, in any case, a French word. Early records show the name Blampoix followed by the word *Aîné*, the correct translation of which is "Elder." To denote seniority in a family business, a Frenchman would use *Aîné*, as indeed Blampoix did, or *Père*, meaning

"Father." Thus, the use of the English word "Senior" in this context is highly unlikely and casts almost total doubt on the suggestion that *B.S.* could have been a Blampoix mark. A far more likely mark for the firm would have been the letters *B.A.* or *B.P.*

Schneider

According to the French Chamber of Commerce directories, Schneider was manufacturing dolls in Paris between 1859 and 1896. In 1865 the firm was advertising porcelain dolls' heads and dolls' bodies of rose-coloured, kid leather, and for much of the lifetime of the company great emphasis was placed on the manufacture of dolls with leather bodies of various types. Schneider's son was registered as a doll maker in 1888 under the official title "Benoist Schneider Jne." We have no record of the father's first name or even of his initial, but, if his son felt it necessary to use the word *Jeune* to distinguish himself from his father, it is almost certain that the father's first name was the same as his own – Benoist. This can only raise the interesting possibility that it was Benoist Schneider who produced the dolls marked *B.S.*

Dolls illustrated on pages 19, 50, 64–5 and 68–9, bear the intials *B.S.* incised on the shoulder-plate; doll J3 (page 128) is also marked in this way.

Clément, Pierre Victor

Originally a shoe-maker, Clément is recorded as working in Paris in 1866–75. In 1866 he obtained a patent for making "embossed," lightweight leather bodies, claiming that these would be more durable than those made of gutta-percha and other materials. An entry in the 1873 Paris directory describes him as: "Maker of dressed dolls; specialist in baptismal dolls. 12 rue Montmorency, Paris". Clément advertised that he made light, strong and jointed bodies in leather. The doll illustrated on page 99 and on page 127 (G2) is an example of the rare pressed-leather body that he patented.

F.G.

When writing of dolls marked *F.G.*, it is almost impossible to separate the names Gaultier and Gesland. Both were in business in Paris over an almost identical period – 1860–1915 – but, as with so many other manufacturers, gaps in the official records make it difficult to give a precise outline of all their business activities. We therefore have the option of merely stating the sparse facts or, taking our courage in both hands and risking the wrath of the purist, combine visual evidence with historical records to produce an educated guess as to the probable origin of dolls marked *F.G.*

Gaultier

French directories record the Gaultier company as operating in Paris between 1860 and 1916. In 1863, under the direction of A. Gaultier, it produced porcelain dolls' heads and doll parts, and in 1878 F. Gaultier exhibited dolls' heads at the Paris Exhibition where he was awarded a silver medal. The company was registered as Gaultier et fils in 1880 and awarded a bronze medal in Brussels, Belgium. Between 1883 and 1900 the company was awarded four silver medals and one bronze medal at international exhibitions and extensively advertised its porcelain dolls' heads and *bébés*.

Gesland

Between 1860 and 1915, Paris directories include the company of Gesland. From 1877 it was located at 5 rue Beranger, Paris, and at different times the name was recorded with the initials "E," "F" and "A." Over the second half of the 19th century Gesland advertised that the company made, exported, distributed and repaired dolls, but

on the shoulder and on the head, is illustrated on pages 60–1, while on pages 38–9 and pages 102–3 are two dolls with *F.G.* incised on the shoulder-plate. Other *F.G.*-style dolls are illustrated on pages 32–3, 46–7 and 50–1. All these dolls have swivel necks, but body styles vary from all wood to all leather.

although it undoubtedly did export, distribute and repair dolls, there are still doubts as to the extent of its doll making activities. There are detailed reports of a "while-you-wait" doll repair service, which operated from shop premises on a 12-hour day, 6-days a week basis.

There is indisputable evidence that Gesland manufactured dolls' bodies both in wood and in stuffed stockinette, and it is known that the company was one of the few manufacturers that often marked bodies with the company name. The fact that many of the bisque heads to be found on Gesland bodies were stamped *F.G.* was originally thought to indicate that both head and body were the product of the Gesland company, but it is now almost certain that the bisque heads stamped *F.G.* were in fact made and supplied by Gaultier.

It has now become clear that Gesland did not make dolls in the full sense. The company certainly produced parts of dolls, assembled dolls, repaired them and offered them for sale, but they might be more accurately described as manufacturers and retailers of doll parts.

Illustrated on pages 44–5, 81 and 88–9 is a doll with *F.G.* incised on the right shoulder and *4* on the back of the head and on the left shoulder; see also page 131 (P3). The doll illustrated on pages 60–1 and 84 has the incised mark *F.G.* on the top-back crown of her head; see also page 124 (B1). A doll described as "F. Gaultier type," with an incised *4*

Huret

The name of Mlle. Huret was first registered in connection with doll making in 1850, and in the following year Leopold Huret is mentioned with a business address at 2 Boulevard des Italiens, Paris. Another, and more permanent, move took place in 1852 when the business address for Huret is recorded as 22 Boulevard Montmartre, Paris. The names of Mlle. Huret and Leopold Huret continue to be recorded together in directories until 1865, when the company name is changed to Huret & Lonchambron.

From 1885 various names are mentioned as having taken over the company, including A. Lemoine, Carette and Prevost, but in 1919 Maison Huret is directly mentioned in advertisements for dolls – and this was only one year before the demise of the company.

Possibly the most important improvement, patented by Huret (in 1861), was the swivel neck, which allowed a doll normal head movement; this patent was taken out some years before Jumeau claimed credit for the invention. Another doll maker in Paris, M. Briens, patented a similar innovation in 1862, but his design had the spherical joint at the *top* of the neck and the head "cut off" immediately below the chin. Researches into French patent records of this time are not made easier by the fact that patents were sometimes registered in the name of the agent, and no

HURET | JUMEAU
MEDAILLE D'OR
PARIS | BÉBÉ JUMEAU |

reference was made to the name of the designer or manufacturer.

The use of metal hands on wooden bodies was also the subject of a Huret patent, and, until they were discontinued in 1890, the firm's articulated, gutta-percha bodies were well promoted by the company and won several medals at various exhibitions.

An all-metal doll, incised *Huret, 56 rue de la Boet*, is illustrated on pages 94–5 and on page 127 (H3); a Huret gutta-percha doll, with an identifying stamp on the chest, is illustrated on pages 92–3. A leather-over-gutta-percha body, also bearing a Huret stamp, is illustrated on pages 36–7. See also page 127 (H1 and H2) and page 132 (R2).

Jumeau

It is recorded that a company known as Belton & Jumeau was producing dolls in 1842 at 14 rue Salle au Comte, Paris; two years later the firm received an honourable mention at the Paris Exhibition. From 1847, however, the company seems to have reverted to the sole control of Pierre Jumeau and was from that time to be found at 18 rue Mauconseil, Paris. During the following twenty years Jumeau dolls received only minor awards, but Jumeau dresses were described as being "very beautiful."

In 1867 Pierre Jumeau moved again to the rue d'Anjou au Marais, where he was joined by his son, Emile, who was to be responsible for dramatically increasing both the quantity and quality of the firm's products.

Pierre Jumeau retired about 1877, four years after a large factory had been opened at Montreuil-sous-Bois. Emile assumed sole charge, a position he retained until the company was absorbed in 1899 into the conglomerate of French doll makers, the Société Française de Fabrication de Bébés et Jouets (S.F.B.J.).

Before 1867 the house of Jumeau had received little recognition or public acclaim. During Emile Jumeau's stewardship it was awarded five gold medals and a silver medal at international exhibitions, and in 1885 Emile was created a Chevalier of the Legion of Honour.

Compared with Bru, the house of Jumeau seems to have obtained comparatively few patents, but, while it might have ignored the attractions of novel innovations, it most certainly produced some of the finest French dolls. However, under the mounting pressure of German competition in the last part of the 19th century, Jumeau, in common with other French manufacturers, was compelled to increase output, sometimes at the expense of quality.

The type of bodies found on dolls produced by the house of Jumeau varied. They included all leather, all wood, leather-over-wood and composition; composition was the most common. Several dolls manufactured in the style of Jumeau are illustrated in this book (see pages 23, 48–9, 50–1 (also 56–7), 52–3, 54–5 and 81); one of the dolls illustrated on pages 34–5 bears the stamp *Jumeau Medaille d'Or*; dolls shown on pages 18–19, 23, 34–5 and 77 are unmarked but probably manufactured by Jumeau.

L.D.

It is unfortunate that the names entered in the French Chamber of Commerce records are often confined to the maker's surname and make no mention of a first name or initial. Many of the doll makers' surnames recorded begin with the letter "D," but the following also have either an initial or first name that begins with "L". They are thus contenders for the *L.D.* mark. Léon Desty, 173 rue du Temple, Paris, was recorded as a doll maker in 1869. Mlle. Léontine Delbosque, appears in the directories between 1876 and 1889 as a doll maker,

exporting dolls in foreign and provincial costume. L. Doléac, 16 rue des Archives, Paris, made dressed and undressed dolls between 1881 and 1908.

Undoubted experts are convinced that it was L. Doléac who marked his dolls with the letters "L.D.," but it is possible that he was not the only doll maker to do so. The doubt arises because these dolls often look as though they date from before 1881–1908, and several have been found wearing original "provincial" costumes, which were a speciality of Mlle. Léontine Delbosque, who was producing dolls between 1876 and 1889. It is possible that two different doll makers might have used the same initials to mark their dolls. This is known to have happened in other cases.

Dolls incised *L.D.* are fairly rare, but two such dolls are illustrated on pages 78–9 and page 108; see also page 125 (C2).

Lavallée-Peronne, Mme.

Mlle. Peronne married in 1865 and became Mme. Lavallée-Peronne with a business address at "A La Poupée De Nuremberg" at 21 rue de Nuremberg, Paris. She is recorded in the directories as working in Paris between 1864 and 1884, and it is known that she had a large shop in that city and that as many as two hundred people worked for her. Labels reading "A La Poupée De Nuremberg/21 rue de Choiseul/Lavallée-Peronne/Trousseaux Complets/Réparations/Paris" were applied to doll's bodies, and in 1870 the company was recorded as being the "only firm recommended by the *Journal des Demoiselles* and *La Poupée Modèle*." The firm specialized in producing dolls' trousseaux, baby linen and children's clothes, and it is likely that the company dressed dolls rather than actually manufacturing them, putting the shop stamp on the dolls' bodies. The doll illustrated on page 132 (Q1) bears a label *Lavallée Peronne* on its chest; on page 84 is illustrated a doll with the shop stamp giving the address at 21 rue de Choiseul. Although it appears that the company did not actually manufacture dolls, or even a major proportion of them, it is included here for completeness.

Rohmer, Marie

The name of Mlle. Marie Antoinette Léontine Rohmer was first recorded in 1857; she operated from a business address at 24 Boulevard Poissonière, Paris. During the same year she obtained a patent that covered articulated joints suitable for dolls with leather bodies.

Like Huret dolls, Rohmer dolls are comparatively rare. They are found with heads made of glazed china or bisque, and they have either painted or glass eyes. Many examples have fixed necks (with the head and shoulder-plate in one piece), although as early as 1858 Rohmer patented plans for a form of swivel head based on a flange joint. This allowed a side-to-side movement but little else.

As far as can be ascertained, the direction of the business remained in the same hands for the twenty-three years of its existence, although, during that time, there were two changes of premises – in 1870 to 23 rue de Choiseul and in 1876 to 178 rue du Faubourg.

The bodies of Rohmer dolls are sometimes stamped on the chest with an oval ink mark (see page 129 (L2) and page 132 (Q2 and Q3). Dolls marked in this way are also illustrated on pages 60–1, 82–3 and 100–1.

Simonne

Paris directories show that the house of Simonne operated in Paris between 1839 and 1878. Some doubt still exists as to the company's manufacturing output, and it is probable that it purchased a large proportion of the parts it used from outside sources.

In 1839 the company functioned from premises at 271 rue St Denis, Paris, but in 1844 it was registered at 5 & 7 Galérie Delorme, Paris. By 1863, however, the company appears to have expanded considerably, for the 1863 directory records it as making dressed dolls and *bébés* at premises at 188 rue de Rivoli, Paris, as well as at 1, 2, 3, 5, 7 & 9 Passage Delorme. In 1867 the firm exhibited mechanical dolls in Paris and won an honourable mention.

There is no record of any doll's head bearing a Simonne mark, but the company's oval blue ink stamp does appear on dolls' bodies, suggesting that, like Lavallée Peronne, Simonne dressed and distributed dolls after assembling heads and bodies bought from other manufacturers. The heads on bodies marked *Simonne* vary from fixed head, to swivel neck and flange neck, while the bodies themselves are all leather (or kid) or leather-over-wood with, sometimes, bisque arms.

Many unmarked heads have been found on bodies that have the Simonne stamp or label. Some of these heads have such a unique and distinct resemblance to each other that collectors often identify a Simonne doll without examining the body. It is possible that these heads were designed and produced by another manufacturer solely for use by Simonne.

Dolls bearing the *Simonne* mark are illustrated on pages 70 and 92–3, and on page 128 (J2 and J3).

IDENTIFYING FASHION DOLLS

The dolls illustrated on the following pages are identified by both a letter and a number – A3, for instance. The letters denote the illustration, the numbers denote position, left to right, within each illustration. The dolls illustrated in colour are coded, so that their body styles may be compared with the undressed examples. The heads on the undressed dolls are not necessarily the same type or style as those on the dressed dolls.

A1 *All-leather body with gussets at elbows, hips and knees.*

A2 *Cloth body with leather arms.*

A3 *All-leather body with gussets at elbows, hips and knees. Bru incised on shoulder-plate.*

B1 *Twill-over-wood body; bisque forearms and lower legs; tenon joints at shoulders, elbows, hips and knees; elbow joint as in R1. F.G. incised on head.*

B2 *Twill-over-carton body; tenon joints at elbows, hips, knees and ankles; elbow joint as in R1. This type of body sometimes has a "Simonne" label.*

C1 *All-leather body with gussets at elbows, hips and knees. The shop stamp on the body reads Recompense/Nadaud/Jouets.*

C2 *All-leather body with bisque arms; tenon joints at shoulders; gussets at hips and knees. L. Déposé D. incised on shoulder-plate.*

C3 *All-leather body; bisque arms and lower legs; one arm bent; no gussets; moulded bosom. R. C. Déposé incised on shoulder-plate. This type of body can also have both arms straight or both arms bent. See also page 73.*

D1, 2 & 3 *"Gesland-type" bodies; stockinette over a padded, articulated metal armature, with wooden support through torso; bisque hands and legs. Sometimes incised F.G. or with a number to indicate size.*

E1 *All-leather body with gussets at hips and knees; separate stitched toes. J. Déposé incised on forehead.*

E2 *All-wood body with tenon joints at shoulders, elbows, wrists, hips, knees and ankles; socket joint at waist.*

E3 *All-leather body with gussets at hips and knees; bisque, Bru breveté-style hands.*

F1 *All-leather body; no gussets; mitten hands.*

F2 *Pink leather from waist down; carton (cardboard) torso to waist. E. Déposé B. incised on shoulder-plate. Underskirt nailed to torso.*

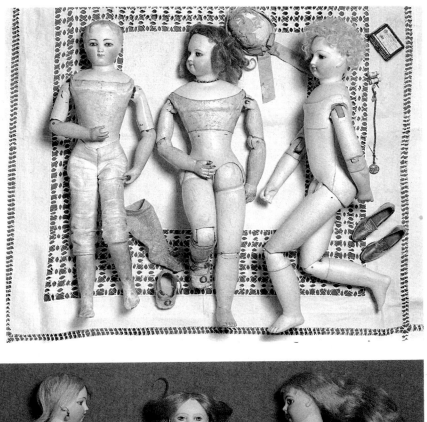

G1 *All-leather body with bisque forearms and metal upper arms; upper legs of unstuffed leather over metal armature; lower legs leather over carton; tenon joints at shoulders; socket joints at elbows. F. Déposé G. incised on shoulder-plate.*

G2 *Rare pressed-leather body, patented by Clément in 1866; tenon joints at shoulders, elbows, hips and knees.*

G3 *Leather-over-wood body with bisque forearms and lower legs; tenon joints at shoulders, elbows, hips and knees.*

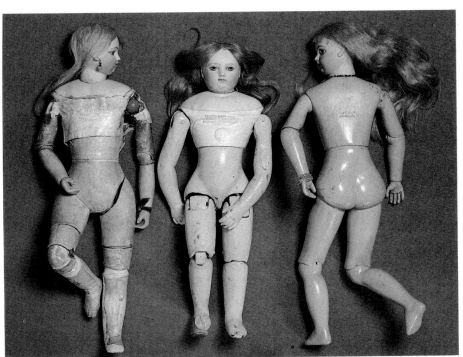

H1 *Leather-over-gutta-percha body with bisque forearms; socket joints at shoulders, elbows and knees. Diagonal-flange hip joints. Huret stamp on chest:* Boulevard Montmartre 22. (Jackie Jacobs)

H2 *Gutta-percha body; tenon joints at shoulders, hips and knees. Huret stamp on chest:* Boulevard Montmartre 22. (Elsie Potter)

H3 *All-metal body with spring fixing; socket joints at shoulders, elbows, wrists, waist, hips and knees.* Huret/56 rué de la Boet *impressed on back.* (Elsie Potter)

I1 *All-leather body with gussets at elbows, hips and knees. Two-faced swivel head: one face with painted "sleeping" eyes, the other with glass eyes. Bru took out a patent for this type of head in 1867.* (Jackie Jacobs)

I2 *All-leather body with bisque forearms; gussets at elbows, hips and knees. Signature of Rochard partly visible through back of shoulder-plate; when held to light, a view of Paris can be seen in the glass pendant inset into shoulder-plate. Patented in 1868.* (Elsie Potter)

J1 *All-leather body with bisque arms; leather-over-wood tenon joints at shoulders and knees; diagonal-flange hip joints. Rare type of body.* (Jackie Jacobs)

J2 *All-leather body with bisque arms; gussets at hips and knees. Simonne body stamp on chest: rue de Rivoli 188.* (Elsie Potter)

J3 *All-leather body with bisque arms; gussets at hips and knees; tenon joints at shoulders. Simonne body stamp on chest; rue de Rivoli 188. B.S. incised on shoulder-plate. The clothes illustrated all belong to this doll.*

K1 *All-wood body; tenon joints at shoulders, elbows, wrists, hips, knees and ankles; flange joints at waist and mid-thighs.*

K2 *All-wood body; tenon joints at shoulders, elbows, hips and knees; socket joints at wrists; flange joints at mid-upper arms and mid-thighs.*

K3 *All-leather body with bisque forearms; leather-over-wood tenon joints at shoulders, elbows and knees; gussets at hips.*

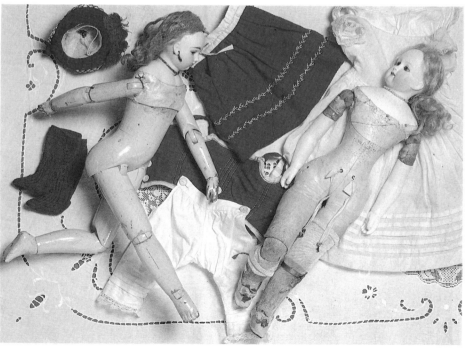

L1 *All-wood body; tenon joints at shoulders, elbows, wrists, hips, knees and ankles; flange joints at waist and mid-thighs.* (Elsie Potter)

L2 *All-leather body with bisque arms; tenon joints at shoulders; socket joints at knees; gussets at hips; metal eyelet holes in torso for stocking support. Oval stamp of Rohmer on torso.* (Elsie Potter)

M1 *All-leather body with bisque arms; gussets at hips.*

M2 *Carton (cardboard) torso with bisque arms and lower legs. Baptême (christening doll); a candy container (see pages 56–7).*

M3 *All-leather body with bisque arms; leather-over-wood tenon joints at shoulders and knees; gussets at hips.*

N1 *All-leather body with gussets at elbows. Incised E.B. on shoulder-plate.*

N2 *All-leather body; no gussets.*

N3 *All-leather body with gussets at elbows and hips.*

O1 *Leather-over-wood body with bisque forearms; tenon joints at shoulders, elbows, hips and knees. Déposé j incised on head/shoulder-plate.*

O2 *All-leather body with wood arms; gussets at hips and knees; tenon joints at shoulders, elbows and wrists. (Untidy repair to hips.)*

O3 *All-wood body; tenon joints at shoulders, elbows, hips and knees; flange joints at waist and mid-thighs. (Waist and leg turned to show versatility.)*

P1 *All-wood body; tenon joints at shoulders, elbows, wrists, hips and knees; flange joints at waist and mid-thighs. (Waist turned to show versatility.)*

P2 *All-leather body with gussets at elbows, hips and knees. B. J^{ne} et Cie incised on one shoulder-plate and F. Déposé on the other. F incised on rear of crown denoting size.*

P3 *All-wood body; tenon joints at shoulders, elbows, hips and knees; socket joints at wrists; flange joints at upper arms and mid-thighs; 4 incised at back of head and on left shoulder; F.G. incised on right shoulder.*

131

Q1 *All-leather body with bisque forearms; kid-over-wood upper arms; gussets at hips; kid-over-wood tenon joints at knees; tenon joints at elbows and shoulders. Label on chest: Lavallée Peronne. 4 incised on head and shoulder.*

Q2 *All-leather body with bisque forearms; gussets at hips and knees; leather-over-wood tenon joints at shoulders and elbows; flange neck joint; head attached by wire running from inside top of head down into body. Green oval Rohmer stamp on body.*

Q3 *All-leather body with bisque forearms; leather-over-wood tenon joints at shoulders; gussets at hips; leather-over-wood socket joints at elbows and knees; flange neck connected as in Q2; metal eyelet holes in torso for stocking support. Green oval Rohmer stamp on torso.*

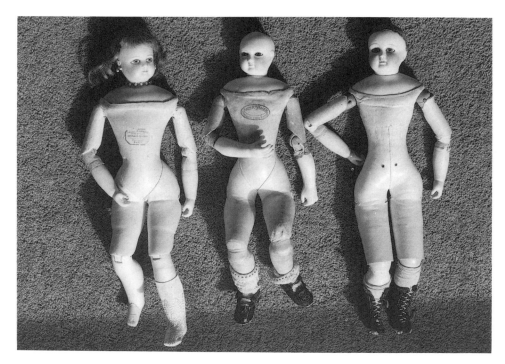

R1 *Leather-over-wood body with bisque forearms; tenon joints at hips and knees; socket joints at shoulders; metal-and-wood tenon joints at elbows (leather has been rolled back to show joint).*

R2 *Gutta-percha body; tenon joints at shoulders, elbows, hips and knees; swivel neck; painted blue eyes. Stamped on chest: Médaille d'Argent/Huret/22 Boulvd Montmartre/Paris/Expon Universelle 1867.*

BUYING AND RESTORING FRENCH FASHION DOLLS

Buying French Fashion Dolls

The long-established collectors or other experts in the field of antique dolls are qualified to buy dolls from any source that offers them for sale. They will quickly discover any faults or defects in a doll – hairline cracks, hidden restoration, incorrect body or body parts – and will be able to ascertain if the clothes are original or even if the doll is a reproduction that has been passed off as an original.

Novices or inexperienced collectors should be far more careful about how and where they purchase a doll. Only time and the constant examination and handling of dolls will enable them to gain experience and acquire the necessary self-confidence to rely on their own judgement.

There are, however, a number of ways in which novices can start to acquire a basic knowledge of the subject. If one exists, join a local doll club. Talk to other people who collect dolls. Visit museums that feature displays of antique dolls. Subscribe to the doll magazines, which contain interesting articles on all types of antique dolls as well as lists of future "doll events." Study books on the subject, and last, but not least, talk to established doll dealers who are specialists in their field. If you explain that you are a novice they will generally be prepared to give you the best advice available and they are probably the best source from which novices can safely buy dolls (see page 134).

In addition to buying from a dealer, antique dolls can be purchased from two other main sources: from a collector who is disposing of an item in his collection or at an auction. Sometimes a collector wishes to sell one or more of his dolls, often because he wishes to "up grade" certain items. This is a perfectly acceptable operation, but novices would be well advised to take certain precautions when buying privately. They should remember that in a private sale they are buying "as seen" and that it might be difficult to obtain satisfaction if defects are discovered later.

In order to avoid such a situation it is always advisable to ask the seller the following questions: Has the doll been restored in any way? Does it have any hairline cracks? Is the head original to the body? Are *all* the body parts original to the body? These questions apply only to dolls with bisque or china heads. The examination of dolls with wood, wax or papier mâché heads is far more complex and not dealt with here. In addition to asking these questions, the buyer should also examine the doll for himself. The wig should be removable to allow a proper examination of the head – in difficult cases it can be safely removed only by steaming – and it should also be possible to examine the body.

If the seller is unable to give satisfactory answers to any of the above questions and if it is not possible to examine the doll thoroughly, it would be unwise to pay the full asking price for the doll. Many collectors are happy to buy a doll that has minor defects, as long as the price paid reflects this; indeed, an enthusiastic collector may be readier than a novice to accept a few blemishes as reflecting the natural hazards the doll encountered during its life. However, an unscrupulous seller may fail to mention the faults when disposing of a doll.

Provided that the price paid for a doll reflects both its qualities and imperfections at the time of purchase, should the owner wish to re-sell later on, he should still expect to gain if the value of all dolls has risen in the intervening period.

Antique dolls may also be bought at auction, and many specialist sales are held each year. The undoubted excitement of participating in these sales is heightened by the hope, especially of the novice, of obtaining a "bargain." Sadly, such hopes are seldom realized.

One of the reasons for this is that, during the actual sale the novice will find himself bidding against one of the following. *Another novice* who, like himself, thinks that the opposing bids are from a more experienced collector and therefore represent a sensible estimate of the doll's value. *A very high reserve* set by the seller, in which case a surprised and delighted auctioneer will take bids "off the wall," and the novice could be the only person in the audience responding. *A doll dealer* who has a special commission from a personal customer prepared to pay a high price to obtain a particular doll. *Doll dealers in general* who earn a living selling dolls and who would not be prepared to see a doll sold at a price substantially below the market one.

In addition to these hazards, the novice should look carefully at the auctioneer's "conditions of sale," which are generally contained in salesrooms' catalogues. They are most revealing. Concerned almost entirely with the rights of the auction house, they are, as far as the buyer and seller are concerned, mainly pre-occupied with limiting or completely removing any rights they might reasonably feel entitled to.

Three final pitfalls face the novice at auction. First, a doll examined before a sale might appear perfect, although the auctioneer will not comment on this, but there is always the risk that it could be mishandled and damaged by one of the many people who will examine it during the preview period. Second, the novice bidder sometimes fails to remember that the "hammer price" does not include the buyer's premium, and this can increase the price of the doll by 10 per cent or more. Finally, it is entirely at the auctioneer's discretion as to how much he increases the amount of the individual bid, and it is very rare that he gives a verbal warning of his intention to do so. An example would be that of a bidder who followed a previous £20 (approximately $28) rise, expecting a similar increase, only to find that, without warning, the bidding increments had leapt to £50 (approximately $70).

The other main source for the purchase of antique dolls is, as has been mentioned, from a dealer who specializes in the trade of dolls and ancillary items. It is strange that, while many long-established and experienced collectors are happy to buy from dealers, novices or less-experienced collectors often go to other sources, usually in the belief that they will buy more cheaply. They may occasionally do so, but, as previously explained, they often meet with disappointing results.

The most important factor protecting the interests of the collector who buys from a dealer is that a dealer is always aware that only by building up a relationship of trust and confidence can he hope to have an on-going business relationship with the collector. This is extremely important to a dealer, as the novice of today could be the enthusiastic collector of tomorrow, and just one "bad deal" could entirely destroy that prospect.

The reputable dealer with worthwhile knowledge of the subject can also give valuable advice in the area in which the collector is particularly interested. He will also generally give a full and honest account of any blemishes a doll may have; these should be reflected in the price paid.

It would be foolish to suggest that a collector could expect to get a real bargain from a dealer. What he should expect to get is a genuine antique doll at a current market price that takes into account the doll's overall condition. This seems to be the business attitude of the majority of dealers, and although there have been regrettable deviations in the past, these have generally been detected and those concerned have suffered accordingly.

Restoring French Fashion Dolls

Very few antique dolls have no imperfections whatsoever. They were produced as playthings for children and often subjected to vigorous handling for many years before becoming prized items in treasured collections. However, any decision to restore or repair such a doll should be very carefully considered before any work is done. It is sad but true that the efforts of enthusiastic amateurs have resulted in dolls with minor imperfections appearing worse after their efforts to restore them than before.

Three important questions should always be asked before any restoration work is started on an antique doll. Does the proposed work concern an imperfection that will get worse if no action is taken? Does the imperfection positively affect the visual appearance of the doll? Is the work involved within the capabilities of the person who intends to do it? If the answer to the first two questions is "no," the necessity for any repair or restoration is doubtful. If the answer to the third question is "no," professional advice should be sought.

There are, however, collectors who feel able and determined to improve a doll, and there are some minor repairs that can be safely effected.

The most beautiful French fashion dolls produced during the second half of the 19th century had bisque heads and, in some cases, bisque forearms and lower legs. Only a real expert is qualified to undertake repairs to bisque, and such repairs should be considered only when the damage is so substantial as to make the doll otherwise valueless. This is especially true as far as the head is concerned. It should also be remembered that work of this nature can seldom be completely concealed, and an expert eye, often aided by an ultraviolet lamp, will generally detect the existence of such repairs. Even so, a repaired head is certainly better than no head at all.

Bisque heads are subject to hairline cracks, which are far from obvious on casual inspection. No doll should ever be purchased unless the seller is prepared to remove the wig to allow a full examination of the head. Bisque-head dolls often have hairline cracks, and it is possible that many such cracks have existed from the time the dolls were made. But this is not always so, and a worthwhile precaution when a fresh crack is discovered is the internal application of a small dab of an epoxy resin at the points to which the crack extends. It is generally possible to arrest any further extension of a fresh hairline crack in this way.

Most fashion dolls were produced with leather bodies; a smaller number have wood, gutta-percha or metal bodies. Any repair to a metal body is best left to a qualified craftsman, although some more gifted amateurs might be capable of doing the work. But some faults and defects in a leather body are well within the scope of the average handyman.

The first problem when working on the body of a fashion doll is gaining access to the damaged area. If this is a leg or an arm, or even the lower torso, there is little difficulty. But if any other part requires attention the dress will have to be removed, and if this is both original and intricate it will involve very delicate handling. Occasionally dresses are stitched into place, in which case it will be almost impossible to gain access to the damaged area. It is possible that the stitching might have occurred early in the doll's life, but there have been cases where this has been done more recently to prevent a proper inspection of a faulty body.

It is absolutely essential that while any work is carried out on the body of a doll great care is taken to protect the head. So, once the dress has been removed, wrap the head securely before starting to work on the body and leave it wrapped until the work is completed.

When one remembers that the majority of the bodies of fashion dolls are more than a hundred years old, some deterioration in the body material is hardly surprising. It often becomes dry and inflexible. The interior stuffing, whether sawdust, powdered cork or horsehair, becomes compacted into a solid mass. In addition, over the years that the doll has spent standing on display, the body has often assumed an ungainly, crouching position.

It is, however, often possible to restore a certain amount of suppleness to leather by the careful use of a micro-crystalline wax. Following the directions on the tin, apply the wax with a sponge and rub it into the whole of the lower part of the doll, paying particular attention to both the front and back of the gusset joints at knee and thigh. After a couple of hours the treatment can be repeated, when it will be found that the leather has regained much of its original elasticity.

To improve the doll's posture, manipulate one joint at a time. Exert gentle pressure to straighten the limb, at the same time pressing both hands towards the gusset; restraint is needed in the amount of pressure applied, as careless handling can result in a split seam or torn leather. Remember, the object of this exercise is to *improve* the posture of the doll and, with care, success can be achieved and sometimes a dramatic improvement results. But always proceed gently and know when to stop. It is almost impossible to make the body as erect as the day it was produced.

After carefully manipulating each joint, it is helpful to lay the body on its back with a protective pad across it. Place a suitable weight, a heavy book for example, on the pad and leave the doll undisturbed for a few days to keep the doll in its new position.

The wax not only restores the suppleness of leather, it also cleans it. Although it will not restore the surface to its original pristine condition, it will usually remove the worst of the ingrained grime.

Damage to leather bodies can also often take the form of a split seam. Action should be taken quickly to limit the extent of the damage. It is not practicable to try to re-sew a seam since, when it was first made, the body was generally sewn on one side and then turned inside-out before being stuffed. If the fault is caught quickly enough, the simplest solution is to apply a little white glue along the line of the seam, overlapping the area of the break.

Only if there is a hole in the leather should the application of a patch be considered. When the size of a hole makes a patch necessary, use an old, cream-coloured kid glove. Do not trim the hole, but use an orange stick to tuck in cotton wool and prevent any further leakage. The patch should be slightly larger than the hole and should be tucked under it so that it lies flat. Apply white glue between the patch and the underside of the hole with a small cotton bud. The hole should not be trimmed because such damage does not always involve any loss of material. When the repair is completed, it is often found that the torn leather of the body can be adjusted to conceal almost completely the patch beneath.

Stuffed leather bodies were often strengthened by an internal wire armature, and occasionally a sharp end of this penetrates and protrudes from the leather. This can sometimes be pushed back into the body together with a small amount of cotton wool to keep it in place and the hole sealed with white glue. If it is not possible to get the armature back into the body, it should be pulled a little way out, and a small length removed with wire-cutters before proceeding to repair the hole in the manner described above.

The aspect that most strongly attracts the collector of fashion dolls is the beautiful gowns they wear. But when such a gown is "original" and a hundred years old, it has seldom fully escaped the ravages of time. Unlike modern dresses, such costumes were created entirely from natural fibres, and they are therefore less able to resist those hazards that are their natural enemy. Extremes in temperature and humidity, exposure to strong light and the appetites of moths and similar creatures are among the hazards, while, over the years, dust will have settled into the fabric, making it stiff and brittle.

It is unfortunate that, in the past, some collectors, faced with an original dress showing visible signs of distress and damage, chose to remove and discard it before replacing it with something similar made in modern materials. Fortunately, this practice has now largely ceased, and when no alternative exists to re-dressing a doll a real effort should be made to find suitable fabrics from a bygone period. Even if the decision is made to re-dress a doll, it is still better not to throw away the original gown. Placed in a transparent envelope it will provide an interesting and historical record for the present and any future owner of the doll.

The direct action that can be taken to improve the appearance of an original fashion gown is limited. Remove the dress only if it is possible to do so without causing further damage. It is advisable that only garments made of cotton are washed. Many collectors claim to have cleaned or washed complete garments successfully, but the risks involved are high and would have to be recognized and accepted by anyone who considered doing the same. It is most certainly not recommended.

One English museum treats old gowns in .the following way. The dress is laid on a flat surface and covered with a muslin mesh, which is stretched on a frame. A hand-held, electric cleaner is then gently passed over the whole surface. The treatment is repeated for the other side of the dress and, if it is possible to do so without endangering the material, the dress is turned inside-out and the process repeated. Although this procedure could not be expected to make any appreciable difference to the brightness of colour, it seems to be a safe way of removing surface dust and dirt as well as any eggs or larvae that might be lurking in the material.

Before attempting to re-sew a burst seam or a tear, the condition of the fabric itself should be closely examined. It is occasionally possible to stitch the fabric, but if the material has become too brittle the pressure of a tightened thread will only cause further damage.

As when carrying out repairs to the body, caution should again be the watchword in any efforts made to improve the condition of the original wardrobe of an antique doll. It is far better to confine such work to defects that cannot be overlooked and that demand skills within the capability of the person who does them.

Occasionally the collector might be offered a fashion doll without clothes of any description – the price asked should reflect this condition, of course. However, the chances that the new owner will find a genuine antique dress, suitable in quality, size and style are extremely small. Yet a person with any needlework talent can find a great amount of enjoyment and satisfaction in making a complete outfit for the doll, although any temptation to use modern fabrics should be sternly resisted. The design itself can be based on those shown in the many illustrated books on 19th-century ladies' fashions, which can still be found in secondhand book shops. Paper patterns are available from a few shops, which also offer a large range of ancillary items for dolls; these should only be used as a general guide, however, and will need to be adapted to suit a particular doll.

A final suggestion that will help to prolong the life of a fashion doll, and particularly its wonderful gowns, is to display the doll only inside a suitable case or dome away from direct light. If artificial light is installed inside the display area it should not be left switched on for long periods. Enclose a sachet or strip of a suitable pesticide with the doll to create an environment guaranteed to preserve the doll for the future.

19TH-CENTURY UNDERWEAR

The underwear worn by French fashion dolls is generally a faithful miniature copy of that worn by fashionable women and girls, made from the same materials and in the same styles. There was, in fact, little difference in the cut of women's and girls' underwear, although the latter was usually plainer and made of tougher materials. Neither the range nor types of garments changed very much between 1860 and 1890, the period covered by the dolls described in this book, despite the very considerable alteration in the style of dresses which took place when the narrow, fitted skirt replaced the wide, full one.

Long cloth, a closely woven cotton, or fairly fine cambric were the usual materials for everyday wear, while finer cotton or lawn was worn on more formal occasions. Linen, which was thicker, less easy to wash and more expensive, was less often used. The trimming was usually self-coloured and restrained: for everyday wear, rather solid, white embroidery edging or insertion was customary, while lace was used with the finer materials. Coloured silk ribbons, threaded through the edging, provided a touch of colour and allowed the fit to be adjusted. Most underwear was made by machine, but the finest would be hand finished.

A set of underwear usually included a chemise, worn under the corset, a pair of drawers, worn over both the chemise and corset, and one or more waist petticoats.

Chemises were usually knee length and straight cut, with the fullness gathered or arranged in neat tucks into a yoke at the neck. On the higher cut ones that were used for day wear there was generally a short, buttoned opening at the centre front. The lower cut chemises, worn with evening dresses, sometimes had a button at the shoulder so that the neckline could be arranged to suit a *décolleté* dress. The buttons were washable, either covered in cotton or made from white china,

resembling pearl. The sleeves, which were set in straight, were very short.

The chemise was worn tucked into the drawers. In the 1860s these reached from waist to knee, but by the 1880s they tended to be longer – mid-calf length – and cut more tightly. They were made with a triangular front waist-band with a channel, through which ran tapes for adjusting the fit at the back. The legs were cut separately, and in wear the fullness of the material would make them overlap at the front and back, so concealing the open crotch and lack of closed gusset. Long and voluminous or very tight skirts and lavatories that were far from today's standards of comfort or hygiene, made this arrangement the only practical one. Only in the 1880s, when standards of hygiene began to improve and active sports became more popular, were knickers with a closed crotch and a gusset introduced. At the same time, combinations – chemise top and drawers cut in one – became increasingly popular because they gave the smooth line at the waist that was better suited to the unwaisted princess-line styles.

Petticoats, which were usually waist length, had waistbands and draw tapes similar to those on the drawers. They were adapted to the shapes of the skirt: in the 1860s, for example, an all-round fullness, gathered into the waist, was usual, while by the end of the decade gored panels were used to give a smoother line. Tucks above the hem and trimming around it helped to give the skirt additional support. Machine pleating was known by the 1860s and became increasingly popular as the century progressed. Flannel petticoats were used to provide additional layers of warmth throughout the century, but it is probable that most of those worn by the dolls that have scalloped edges and herringbone embroidery are late 19th century. Some petticoats had attached bodices. Most of these were intended for children, but they were also

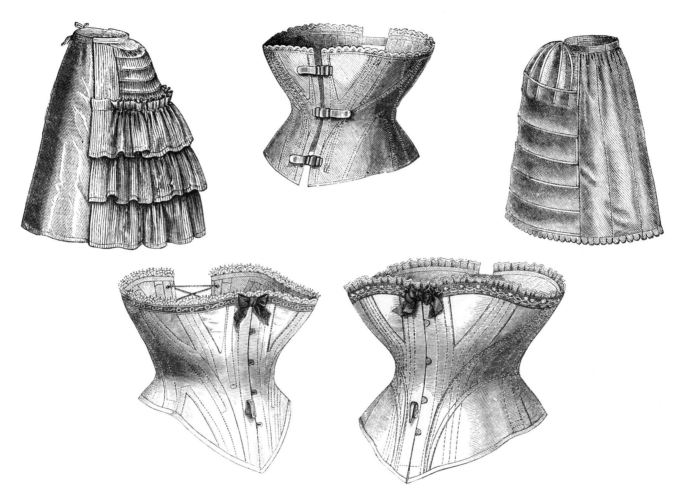

worn by adults, as an alternative to the fitted, front-fastening, hip-length camisole or corset cover, with lightweight and semi-transparent dresses.

The main exceptions to the precise miniaturization of styles of underwear from the fashion dolls were many of the corsets. Full-sized corsets were made from the same kind of materials and boned in a similar fashion and with the same form of eyelet, but, unlike the miniatures, full-sized corsets were always shaped to the figure with gussets at the bust and curves at the hips. They also fastened with a front busk (stiffener), the back lacing being used mainly to adjust size. This discrepancy is interesting, because corsets on 18th- and early 19th-century dolls are much closer copies of the full-sized garment.

M. B. Ginsburg

GLOSSARY

Almond-eyed: term used to describe a doll with almond-shaped holes cut in its head for the insertion of eyes.

Applied ears: ears made in separate moulds and attached to the doll's head before the first firing of the bisque.

Armature: the internal framework of wire, metal or wood that is used to assist in maintaining a doll's posture.

Articulated: term used to describe a doll with joints allowing the various limbs to move.

Automaton (pl. automata): a figure or toy that has some form of movement activated by mechanical means.

Baptême: a type of doll, patented in 1865 by Felix Egrefeuil, that contained *dragées* (sugar almonds) in its carton (cardboard) torso.

Bébé: term usually used to refer to a doll that has the proportions of a young child and a shorter, fatter body than a lady doll.

Bisque (sometimes known as biscuit): a ceramic material that can be poured into a mould or pressed before being fired at a high temperature. Generally painted before further firing at a lower temperature. It has an unglazed, matt surface.

Breveté (French): patented; (*breveté* is a male patentee, *brevetée* a female patentee).

Character dolls: dolls with unusual faces, sometimes portrait faces, of a kind not usually found on fashion dolls.

China head: term used to describe a head of glazed porcelain, a ceramic material that was widely used for dolls' heads before being superseded by bisque in the second half of the 19th century.

Composition: the name given to a number of substances (including papier mâché) used to make dolls' bodies; it was usually made of wood pulp and an adhesive of some kind.

D.E.P. or Déposé (French) or Deponiert (German): letters incised in the bisque shoulder-plate or head of a doll to indicate that the manufacturer's trade mark or patent had been registered.

Fired-in-bisque: a term used to describe the process by which the tints used to colour a doll's head were painted on the bisque after the first, but before the second, firing. The second firing, at a lower temperature than the first, sets the paint.

Fixed neck: the term used to describe the head mounting in which there is no joint between the head and shoulder-plate, which are made in one piece.

Flange joint: the term used to describe the joint formed by two flat surfaces held in place by a retaining ridge and a central cord or pin.

Flange neck: the term used to describe a joint that allows side-to-side movement of a doll's head; it is formed by the two flat surfaces of the head and neck, which are held in place by a ridge.

Gusset: a piece of material let into another piece of fabric to enlarge or strengthen it.

Gussetted body: a leather or fabric body with insets at some or all joints – shoulders, elbows, wrists, hips, knees, ankles – to allow movement.

Gutta-percha: a tough, greyish-black substance obtained from the latex of Malaysian trees; it resembles rubber but tends to become brittle with age. It was used in the 1880s to make dolls' bodies and heads.

Incised marks: marks, generally numbers or letters, that are incised into the bisque of a doll's head or shoulder-plate, sometimes both. Bisque heads and shoulder-plates were generally marked by the factory that produced them; only large doll making companies could afford their own works and, therefore, dolls' heads that were unique to themselves.

Intaglio eyes: painted eyes, in which the details of iris and pupil have been engraved.

Jointed body: an alternative term for articulated body (*qv*).

Mannikin (or manikin): a dummy figure used to display costume; also an artist's lay figure.

Pandora: a mannikin or doll, generally no taller than about 36 inches (90cm), used to display costumes.

Papier mâché: a paper pulp, combined with a whitening agent and a suitable glue, that was used for the manufacture of dolls' heads and bodies in the early 19th century. At the end of the 19th century a new type of papier mâché, which could be poured into a mould rather than having to be pressure moulded, was developed; it was stronger and more durable than the earlier mixture.

Parisienne: an alternative name for a fashion doll, first used by Emile Jumeau to describe the bisque-head fashion doll produced by his company. The word is used by some collectors instead of the phrase "fashion doll."

Pate: the crown of the head; the term is also used to describe the piece of cork or cardboard that was used to cover the hole made in the crown of some dolls' heads and to which the wigs were attached.

Shoulder-head: the terms used to describe the head mounting of a doll when the head and shoulders are moulded as one piece.

BIBLIOGRAPHY

Arnold, J., *Patterns of Fashion, volume 2, 1860–1939*, Macmillan, London, 1968

Blum, S. (ed) *Fashions from Harper's Bazaar, 1860–1890*, Dover, London, 1978

Borger, Mona, *Chinas*, Borger Publications, 1983

Byford, Peggy (Pegby), *The Wooden Doll*, Key Books, 1984

Cieslik, Jürgen and Marianne, *German Doll Encyclopaedia, 1800–1939*, Hobby House Press Inc., Maryland, 1985; White Mouse Publications, London, 1985

Coleman, Dorothy, S., Elizabeth A. and Evelyn J., *The Collector's Encyclopedia of Dolls*, Crown Publishers Inc., New York, 1968; Robert Hale, London, 1970. (Volume 2 is in preparation, publication 1986)

Coleman, Dorothy S., Elizabeth A. and Evelyn J., *The Collector's Book of Dolls' Clothes*, Crown Publishers Inc., New York, 1975; Robert Hale, London, 1976

Coleman, Dorothy S., *Lenci Dolls*, Hobby House Press Inc., Maryland, 1977

Foulke, Jan, *Simon & Halbig Dolls – The Artful Aspect*, Hobby House Press Inc., Maryland, 1984

Gerken, Jo Elizabeth, *Wonderful Dolls of Wax*, Calico Print Shop, Wichita, Kansas, 1964

Gerken, Jo Elizabeth, *Wonderful Dolls of Papier Mâché*, Doll Research Associates, Lincoln, Nebraska, 1970

Gibbs Smith, C. H., *The Fashionable Lady in the 19th Century*, Her Majesty's Stationery Office, London, 1964

Ginsburg, Madeleine, *Victorian Dress in Photographs*, Batsford, London, 1982

Hart, Luella, *Complete French Doll Directory*, Oakland, California, 1965

Hillier, Mary, *The History of Wax Dolls*, Hobby House Press Inc., Maryland, 1985; Souvenir Press Ltd, London, 1985

King, Constance Eileen, *A Collector's History of Dolls*, Robert Hale, London, 1977

King, Constance Eileen, *Jumeau*, Hobby House Press Inc., Maryland, 1983

Noble, John, *A Treasury of Beautiful Dolls*, Hawthorn Books, New York, 1971

Parry-Crooke, Charlotte (ed), *Toys-Dolls-Games*, Hastings House Publishers, New York, 1981; Denys Ingram, London, 1981

Pollock's Toy Museum, *Pollock's Dictionary of English Dolls*, Robert Hale, London, 1982

Richter, Lydia, *The Beloved Käthe-Kruse Dolls*, Hobby House Press Inc., Maryland, 1983

Rothstein, N. (ed), *Four Hundred Years of Fashion*, Victoria & Albert Museum/Collins, London, 1984

Whitton, Margaret, *The Jumeau Doll*, Dover Publications, New York, 1980

INDEX

Numbers in *italics* refer to captions to illustrations